Somerset MURDERS

Nicola Sly & John Van der Kiste

First published in 2008 by Sutton Publishing Limited

Reprinted in 2010 by
The History Press
The Mill, Brimscombe Port,
Stroud, Gloucestershire, GL5 2QG
www.thehistorypress.co.uk

Reprinted 2012

Copyright © Nicola Sly & John Van der Kiste, 2010

All rights reserved. No part of this publication may be reproduced, stored in a retrieval system, or transmitted, in any form, or by any means, electronic, mechanical, photocopying, recording or otherwise, without the prior permission of the publisher and copyright holder.

Nicola Sly & John Van der Kiste have asserted the moral right to be identified as the authors of this work.

British Library Cataloguing in Publication Data
A catalogue record for this book is available from the British Library.

ISBN 978 0 7509 4795 4

Typesetting and origination by Sutton Publishing
Printed and bound in England.

CONTENTS

	Authors' Note & Acknowledgements	v
1.	'Good people, pray for me!' *Hemington, 1740*	1
2.	'I hope God and the world have forgiven me' *Over Stowey, 1789*	5
3.	'I am entirely innocent' *Buckland St Mary, 1823*	11
4.	'There are thieves in the house!' *Bath, 1828*	17
5.	'Not a fortnight longer! Mark my words' *Withypool, 1829*	22
6.	'Here's a pretty bitch coming down the lane' *Chard, 1829*	26
7.	'Neither a murder nor a mystery' *Over Stratton, 1830*	33
8.	'I can't bear to see it!' *Sandpit Hill, near Langport, 1835*	37
9.	Bare-Knuckle Fight at the Running Horse *Yeovil, 1843*	41
10.	'What Martha's already said goes for nothing' *Crewkerne, 1843*	45
11.	'It's no use, I've done it' *Weston-super-Mare, 1844*	52
12.	'Ask her first if she believes in God?' *Bath, 1851*	58
13.	'I did it for love' *Frome, 1851*	63

14.	'We'll find the body yet' *Simonsbath, 1858*	67
15.	'Nothing has ever been administered to her in her food' *Yeovil, 1860*	73
16.	'No one knew of my intention' *Rode, 1860*	77
17.	'Spare my wife' *Dundry, 1861*	85
18.	A Policeman's Lot *Yeovil, 1862*	90
19.	'Goodnight' *Ridgehill, 1883*	95
20.	'Yes, I done it!' *Henstridge, 1883*	99
21.	'You ought to be hanged' *Yeobridge, 1889*	103
22.	'You will have me here for something more serious than this' *North Petherton, 1913*	106
23.	'What's the use of bamboozling about it?' *Porlock, 1914*	112
24.	'Go on, put down what you like' *West Hatch, 1933*	116
25.	'I shall be glad when the old bastard is out of the way' *Bath, 1933*	121
26.	'Stop worrying. It is all right' *Milborne Port, 1943*	126
27.	'Thank you' *Middlezoy, 1947*	131
28.	'One of the most terrible cases of murder I have known' *Wembdon, Bridgwater, 1950*	134
29.	'That is a frame-up, that is' *Bath, 1951/2*	137
30.	'The strife is o'er, the battle won' *Loxton, 1954*	144
	Bibliography & References	*149*
	Index	*152*

AUTHORS' NOTE & ACKNOWLEDGEMENTS

In researching accounts of true crime from earlier centuries, there are often minor discrepancies between different accounts, especially with regard to proper names. Jane Buttesworth, killed in 1740, is sometimes given as Jane Buttersworth, while her contemporary is alternatively recorded as Ann James and Ann Somers. Jane Walford, murdered in 1789, is sometimes named Jenny, and her husband John's mother is also referred to on occasion as his stepmother. The factory where Joan Turner, murdered in 1829, used to work, was variously reported as Rist's, Risk's or Riste's. Perhaps the greatest variation of all concerns the man hanged for the murder of Emma Davies in 1889. We have preferred the name Samuel Reyland, though it has also appeared as Reynald, Rylands and even Reynolds.

While writing this book, we have relied heavily on the work of previous authors in the field, all of whose relevant works are listed in the bibliography, as well as local and national newspapers, via microfilm and the internet. We would also like to acknowledge the assistance of the staff of the Somerset Local Studies Library; the Hope Inn, Bridgwater; and the White Hart Inn, Somerton.

Particular thanks are due to Richard Sly and John Higginson, Nicola's husband and father, Kim and Kate Van der Kiste, John's wife and mother, for their encouragement, advice, reading through the manuscript in draft form and assistance with the photography, and Mike Clapperton, for the provision of the photograph on page 107. Finally, particular thanks go to our editors at Sutton Publishing; Simon Fletcher, Matilda Pearce and Michelle Tilling.

1

'GOOD PEOPLE, PRAY FOR ME!'

Hemington, 1740

Murders committed by women are comparatively rare, and those perpetrated by a mother and daughter pairing are almost unheard of, yet in 1740, a young servant girl was cruelly beaten to death by her mistress and her mistress's daughter. The mother and daughter killers were Elizabeth and Betty Branch, who lived at Hemington, near Frome in East Somerset. Elizabeth originally came from a well-to-do Bristol family, her father an ex-surgeon, who had become a ship's captain. She had been a singularly bad-tempered, violent child and, throughout her childhood, had been constantly warned by her mother that she would never find a husband if she continued to behave so terribly. However, despite her evil disposition, Elizabeth somehow managed to attract the attentions of a prosperous lawyer, Benjamin Branch.

They married and, in due course, Elizabeth gave birth to two children, a daughter, Betty, and a son, Parry. Elizabeth ruled the household with a rod of iron and, so brutal and sadistic was her treatment of the servants that it became almost impossible to find anyone willing to work in the Branch home. The gentle Benjamin was appalled and sickened by his wife's cruelty – he died at an early age, sparking rumours among local gossips that his wife had poisoned him.

While Parry seemed to take after his father in his demeanour, Betty was truly her mother's daughter. Mother and daughter bullied, tormented and physically abused the unfortunate servants who worked for them in their home. Once they beat a servant so severely that he lost control of his bowels, after which he was forced to eat his own excrement. Sadly, their extreme ill-treatment of their staff ultimately resulted in the tragic death of one of them, a homeless orphan named Jane Buttesworth.

Jane, who was then about 12-years-old, went to work for the Branch family in September 1739, her services having been arranged for the family by John Lawrence of Bristol. She started her new employment at the same time as another girl, Ann Somers and, while Ann was spirited and down-to-earth, more than capable of standing her corner, Jane was an altogether different type of girl. Having been told by Lawrence that she had been irrevocably apprenticed to the family, the meek and mild Jane resigned herself to her fate and tried her hardest to please her difficult employers, but her life was made a misery as, over the next few months, she was repeatedly verbally and physically chastised for making the slightest error. Ann often tried to protect her fellow servant, but was sharply told to mind her own business and threatened with similar punishments.

Matters came to a head on Tuesday 12 February 1740, when young Jane was sent to the village of Faulkland, half a mile away, on an errand to buy barm (a raising agent containing yeast cells and used for bread making and brewing) from Anthony Budd. She returned without the barm, telling her mistress that there was none for sale, but she had not bargained on William Budd, the son of the merchant, arriving at Highchurch Farm the very next day to help Parry chop wood. Mrs Branch asked William why his father had had no barm on the previous day, to which William replied that there had been plenty of barm but no customers. Jane was summoned to explain herself and swore that she was telling the truth, but Mrs Branch's anger was not to be placated. Ann Somers was promptly dispatched to see Mr Budd in order to determine the truth of the matter.

Arriving at Budd's house, Ann was met by Mrs Budd who assured her that Jane Buttesworth had not called to buy barm on the previous day. When this information was relayed to Betty Branch, she flew into a rage and began to beat the unfortunate Jane around the head with her fists and pinch her ears. She then ordered the girl into the kitchen, where she met with Elizabeth, who picked up a stout stick from a windowsill. Betty flung Jane to the floor, kneeling on her neck while her mother beat the poor girl until the blood poured through her clothes, deaf to her screams of pain and the frantic protests of Ann Somers. Next, Betty removed one of Jane's shoes and beat the poor girl with the heel until she was 'quite mazed and unable to stand'.

Finally, Jane managed to free herself as Betty stood up with the intention of delivering a few kicks to the servant girl's prone body. Jane staggered out of the kitchen and into the hall but was soon recaptured and dragged back to the kitchen. There she was ordered to wash away the copious blood with which she was now covered, but almost as soon as she tried to obey, she collapsed in a swoon. An exasperated Mrs Branch ordered her to dust and sweep the parlour and Jane struggled to comply. However, when Ann felt safe enough to go to the parlour to check on her, she found the sobbing girl leaning dazedly on her broom, weak from loss of blood and too dizzy to move.

Ann ran to tell Mrs Branch that Jane was seriously hurt and needed help, but Elizabeth merely laughed, calling Ann a 'Welsh bitch' and saying that if Jane did not pull herself together and get on with her work she would get another beating. Ann half-carried Jane out into the yard so that she could get a breath of fresh air, but there she met Betty who threw a bucket of icy water over the two servants. Despite Ann's protests that Jane was unable to work, Mrs Branch insisted that work she must, otherwise she would break her neck. By then it was time for Ann to milk the cows, which left Jane alone at the mercy of her malevolent mistresses.

When Ann returned from milking, she found Jane lying on the floor of the brew house, drifting in and out of consciousness. Ann helped her into a chair, but she was immediately reproached by Betty, who told Jane that if she did not get on with her work, then she would have salt rubbed into her wounds. Jane mumbled, 'I will, Miss,' but, despite her apparent willingness she was physically unable to comply with Betty's demands. At her inaction, Betty promptly carried out her threat, pushing Jane to the floor and rubbing salt into the numerous cuts on the maid's body. Jane continued to mutter, 'I will, Miss,' until eventually she was dragged into the kitchen and dressed in a clean cap, to hide the wounds on her head.

She was left to lie on the kitchen floor until early evening, when Ann tried to rouse her. Unable to wake her, Ann soon realised that Jane would never wake again and rushed to tell Mrs Branch that she was dead, but Elizabeth denied it, telling Ann to put her to bed so that she could recover. Ann and Jane usually shared a bed in the servants' quarters and, when the day's work was done, Ann was forced to spend an uncomfortable night with a rapidly stiffening corpse as a bedfellow.

After an (understandably) sleepless night, Ann again went to Mrs Branch. By now, Jane lay cold in her bed, and Elizabeth reluctantly acknowledged that the young girl was dead. Her body lay ignored all day, and on the following morning, William Budd was sent to Frome to procure a shroud and coffin. Ann was forced to attend to the corpse, instructed by Mrs Branch to wash away the dried blood from Jane's body. Mrs Branch took away her blood-soaked clothes and concealed them in the apple store, wrapping the dead girl in the shroud to conceal her terrible injuries.

Jane's body was buried in the churchyard of Hemington Church on the following Sunday, four days after the fatal beating. However, Mrs Branch aroused suspicion at the burial when she refused to let anyone see the body and repeatedly questioned the sexton, Francis Coombes, about the depth of the grave. As rumours spread throughout the village, two local men decided to dig up the corpse to determine the truth behind Jane's sudden death.

Under the pretext of wanting to do some bell ringing, Robert Carver and John Marchant obtained a key to the church. On Wednesday 20 February, they exhumed the coffin of Jane Buttesworth and, with several other willing helpers, carried it into the church. Removing the long nails that secured the lid, they asked several of the village women to look at the body. Peeling back the shroud, all were appalled at the extent of Jane's injuries and, locking the church door behind them, the men sought out churchwarden John Craddock and told him what they had found.

The police were summoned and Jane's body was examined by a surgeon, who determined that she had died from blood loss as a result of her injuries, which included a fractured skull. Barely an inch of her body was not covered with bruises and, in the opinion of the surgeon, she had been 'so barbarously and inhumanely used that it was enough to kill the stoutest man'. The Branch family, Ann Somers and John Lawrence, were immediately arrested on suspicion of her murder and detained at the nearby Faulkland Inn. A search of the Branch's home revealed the bloody sticks used to beat Jane to death.

At the coroner's inquest, held on 22 and 23 February, Ann Somers made a statement giving her account of the events leading up to Jane's death. Her statement was supported by that of William Budd and as a result, Elizabeth and Betty Branch were committed to trial for the murder of their young employee. Proceedings opened at the Somerset Assizes on 31 March 1740. Elizabeth Branch, a woman of considerable means following the death of her husband, employed no less than eight lawyers to defend her, but her only real defence was her claim that all the prosecution witnesses were liars who had falsely accused her of murder in order to obtain money from her. When that argument failed to impress the judge, it was then alleged that Jane suffered from fits and had sustained her injuries falling down with a pail of water. It was next suggested that Ann Somers was responsible for causing Jane's wounds or that the injuries had been made when the body was exhumed.

After six hours of listening to the evidence, the trial jurors came to their decision within minutes, without finding it necessary to withdraw from the court to deliberate. A verdict of guilty was passed on both Elizabeth and Betty Branch, at which Betty collapsed, remaining unconscious for some forty-five minutes. When warders tried to revive her with a drink, they were chided by her mother who cried out that it would be better to let her die there than live to be hanged.

The women received the obligatory death sentence and were promptly dispatched to Ilchester Gaol to await their execution, set for 3 May. Although Elizabeth petitioned for a reprieve as a matter of course, she showed little interest in the proceedings, seeming more concerned with discovering the facts about hanging and the positioning of the noose. Betty at least appeared to show some remorse and, on occasions, was permitted to leave the gaol in the company of a warder who took her to his house in nearby Limington. She expressed a desire to be buried in the pretty little churchyard at Limington after her execution, but her wish was eventually denied.

Once all hope of a reprieve was lost, Elizabeth Branch requested that the execution should take place in the early morning, in the hope that the early hour would deter the arrival of many spectators. However, when the execution party arrived at the site, it was to discover that part of the gallows had been destroyed. Anxious to get the hanging over as soon as possible, Elizabeth suggested that a nearby tree could be used, but the gibbet was quickly repaired and, having learned the mechanics of hanging while incarcerated, Elizabeth herself fitted the noose around her daughter's neck.

Elizabeth Branch's address to the few spectators who had braved the early morning was a mixture of remorse and excuses for her crime. She admitted to striking her maid, but argued that since this was not done with the intention of killing her, then the sentence passed upon her was unjust. Her biggest regret seemed to be that her behaviour had rubbed off on Betty, bringing her to the gallows to face the same punishment. Betty also made a speech in which she rued being trained while young to follow the paths of cruelty and barbarity. She asked that her unhappy end act as a warning to others to avoid like crimes and entreated the small crowd; 'Good people, pray for me!'

The bodies of Elizabeth and Betty Branch were interred in Ilchester churchyard. Tragically, it came to light only after her murder that the unfortunate Jane Buttesworth had indeed fulfilled her final errand and had called at the Budd's premises to buy barm, as requested. Although Margaret Budd had initially insisted that Jane had not called, it emerged that the girl had been sent on her errand without any money and had been refused credit by Mrs Budd. It speaks volumes of Elizabeth Branch's legendary temper that Jane felt unable to mention this fact as she was being viciously beaten to death for her failings, and that Margaret Budd had been so afraid of the consequences of denying the girl credit that she had told a lie which ultimately led to the horrific death of an innocent child.

2

'I HOPE GOD AND THE WORLD HAVE FORGIVEN ME'

Over Stowey, 1789

In the Quantock hills, high above the village of Over Stowey, threre is a well-known and popular beauty spot. However, its sinister name suggests anything but beauty. Since a shocking event that occurred there over two centuries ago, it has always been known as 'Dead Woman's Ditch'.

In 1765, John Walford was born at Over Stowey, the son of a collier (as the makers of charcoal from wood were then known). He grew up to be a good-looking, popular, even-tempered young man, and followed his father into the charcoal business, sometimes supplementing his income by working as a casual farm labourer in the summer. When he fell in love, the object of his affections could be said to have been a cut above the illiterate but hardworking manual worker. Ann Rice, who came from the neighbouring village of Nether Stowey, was the youngest of four daughters of a prosperous miller and his wife. She and John were very much in love and there was an understanding between them that one day they would be married.

The trade of charcoal maker was a lonely one, with little free time for courting. John spent most of the week living in the woods, in a makeshift shelter that he had constructed from poles and turf, rarely coming into contact with other people. He cut and collected timber, then closely supervised it as it burned in a turf-covered pit. The pit remained alight for four or five days, during which time it needed tending every couple of hours, and when he could snatch a little sleep, John simply curled up fully clothed on a bed of straw in his hut. His only food during the week was bread and cheese, his only drink, water from the streams. Every Monday he would carry a half-peck loaf weighing almost 9lbs and 2lbs of cheese into the forest for sustenance. He returned home every Saturday night to eat a hot meal, drink with his friends and catch up with some much needed sleep, before attending church on Sundays.

Into John's isolated life came Jane Shorney, the daughter of another charcoal burner. She was described as 'a poor stupid creature, almost an idiot; yet possessing a little kind of craftiness…an ordinary squat person, disgustingly dirty, and slovenly in her dress.' Jane set her cap at John and took to deliberately

Dead Woman's Ditch. (© Nicola Sly)

seeking him out in the woods while she was supposed to be gathering wood for the fire. For a lonely and virile young man, totally devoid of female company, the outcome of her visits was almost inevitable. She gave birth to a son in 1785 and named John as the baby's father. John was soon taken into custody by the parish officers and given an ultimatum; he must either marry Jane or pay for the child's support. His mother, Ann, stepped in and offered to help, thus effectively letting John off the hook. In the following year Jane gave birth to a daughter, allegedly fathered by John's brother, William.

Ann Rice was obviously prepared to forgive and forget, as the banns were read for her marriage to John in 1787. However, John's mother, who until then had approved of the match between her son and his socially superior girlfriend, now seemed jealous that Ann was replacing her in John's affections. Having previously welcomed the girl into her home, she suddenly took a violent dislike to her; a situation not helped by the fact that Ann's father, George, had relinquished his mill, and as a result lost some of his income and social standing. Perhaps she threatened to withdraw her support of John's illegitimate child, or maybe he simply did not want to go against his mother's wishes, but the engagement between John and Ann Rice was broken off and Ann went into service. However, she continued to meet John secretly and eventually she too became pregnant.

Meanwhile, no doubt heartened by the news of his broken engagement, Jane Shorney resumed her prolonged seduction of John. When she was expecting his second child, John had no choice but to marry her.

The wedding took place on 18 June 1789 and, once married, 24-year-old John took a new job as a husbandman, which left him free to return home to his wife every night at the cottage they shared in the nearby village of Biscombe. Although their union seemed peaceful on the surface, John felt so trapped by his marriage that he was soon contemplating either moving to London or emigrating to a foreign country. It was only a lack of ready money that kept him tied to Somerset and to a wife he resented, but he planned to sell his horse and his bed in order to raise funds to leave. According to William Bishop, a friend of John's who had given Jane away at their wedding, John told him that he would sooner see the Devil in his house than his new wife, saying, 'I must either murder her or go from her.' Jane, it is said, constantly taunted her husband about his true love, Ann, and her spiteful remarks and constant criticism of him made his life a misery.

Jane got into the habit of visiting either her mother or her nearby neighbours for long periods of time, leaving John alone in the house to brood. On 5 July, only three weeks after his wedding, he came home and once again found his wife absent. He went next door to see if she was with their neighbours and to pick up his door key, and was invited in for supper, passing a couple of hours with the Rich family before going home to wait for his wife. On her return, she suggested a visit to the Castle of Comfort public house in the nearby village of Doddington to buy cider. John gave her a shilling from his weekly wage of 6*s* to do so, but as she was afraid of walking in the dark and reluctant to go alone, Jane persuaded him to accompany her. He returned home alone at 12.30 a.m. the following morning, and he was observed creeping barefoot through the darkness by two of the Rich sisters who were waiting up for another sister.

The Castle of Comfort Inn, Doddington. (© Nicola Sly)

Early the following morning, two children noticed blood running from beneath a gate. They reported their find to two men who lived nearby, and soon the body of Jane Walford was found at the place now known as Dead Woman's Ditch.

When told of the gruesome discovery, John expressed shock and surprise. He was asked to view the body but declared that he could not bear to see it, so he set off in the opposite direction towards his mother-in-law's house, where he persuaded her to accompany him to the gruesome site. Arriving at the scene of the murder, he glanced briefly at the corpse before staggering back in distress. Questioned by a local businessman, Thomas Poole, Walford maintained that his wife had left their cottage the previous evening to buy cider. He was asked to search the body to see if the coin he had given her was still there and, having first been reluctant to approach his dead wife, eventually made a great show of searching her pockets for the shilling. When it could not be found, he suggested that his wife had been attacked and robbed. However, his actions that morning aroused considerable suspicion.

On leaving his house to view the body, he met his brother William, whom he told that his wife had 'cut her throat'. This detail had not yet been mentioned to the widower, and was something he would not have known if he had played no part in Jane's demise. A search of Walford's cottage produced a small bloodstained pocket knife. The breeches that he had been wearing on the previous night were also heavily stained with blood and there, forgotten in the pocket, was a shilling. A pair of mud-stained stockings was found concealed between the ceiling and thatch of the cottage.

Walford was questioned about his clasp knife, which he claimed to have lent to his brother, William. The latter vehemently denied this and immediately Walford changed his story, saying that he had given the knife to a little boy whose name he could not remember. The knife was found on the following day, bearing traces of dried blood, concealed beneath a window seat in the cottage.

Although he initially denied killing Jane, the evidence against Walford was overwhelming and he soon confessed to her murder. During their trip to the Castle of Comfort Inn, Jane had provoked yet another argument and pushed him too far. Ever mindful of having forsaken his beloved Ann for this nagging harridan, something inside him finally snapped. He grabbed her by the throat and shook her, then grabbed a post from a hedge and beat her until she fell unconscious, fracturing her skull in the process. Finally he pulled out a knife and slit her throat. Realising that he had killed her, he tried to drag her body to a disused mineshaft but, finding the pregnant corpse too heavy to move, he eventually left it in the ditch. Having first retrieved the shilling that he had given her earlier, he then proceeded to conceal Jane's body, covering it with stones, branches and leaves.

In the light of his confession to the murder, John's subsequent trial at Bridgwater, which opened on 18 August 1789, lasted only three hours before he was officially pronounced guilty and sentenced to death. The presiding judge, Lord Chief Justice Kenyon, was clearly sympathetic towards the prisoner, whom he appeared to view as a quiet and decent man pushed beyond his limits. While Walford showed no emotion, Kenyon wept as he pronounced the death sentence but, despite his obvious reticence, he was under pressure from local residents to

Memorial to Jane Walford at Doddington. (© Nicola Sly)

punish Walford and deliver the ultimate penalty. Jane's murder came at a time when there had been several violent crimes in the area in the preceding few years. The community demanded that John Walford should be made an example of, asking that he should be hung from a gibbet at the place where his wife's body was found, his body subsequently caged and left for all to see. This, they felt, would act as a deterrent to anyone else contemplating violence in the future.

Accordingly, next day John was shackled around his neck, wrists and ankles and taken by cart to the execution site. A crowd of almost 3,000 villagers gathered to watch the hanging, but on John's arrival at Dead Woman's Ditch, it became apparent that the construction of the gibbet was not yet finished. He was taken to a nearby inn, The Globe at Nether Stowey, for a drink of ale and a meal of bread while the preparations for his death were completed.

As he waited, the crowd parted and a lone young woman approached the prisoner. It was John's first love, Ann Rice. Out of respect, the majority of the crowd turned their backs as a member of the execution party assisted her onto the cart. The couple were allowed to talk for a few minutes before Ann leaned forward, intending to give John a farewell kiss. The executioner would not allow this and placed his arm between them, and then lifted Ann gently from the cart.

John joined in a recital of the Lord's Prayer and the Apostles' Creed before finally confessing his guilt to the assembled crowd. He admitted murdering his wife but swore that the murder was done 'without foreintending it.' He then said, 'I hope God and the world have forgiven me', before a brisk slap to the horse's rump set the cart in motion, leaving his body dangling by the neck at the rope's end.

Leigh Woods, near Bristol.

John's body was subsequently caged and hoisted to the top of the 30ft-high gibbet, where it remained as an example to others until exactly a year to the day after the murder, when the cage finally fell to the ground. Cruelly, this spectacle was within clear view of John's childhood home where his parents still lived. Every time they opened their front door, they were greeted by the sight of their son's body, slowly decaying as the days passed by. Ravaged by crows and blowflies, his remains were eventually buried, still in their metal cage, at the foot of the gibbet. The execution site is still marked on maps of the area as 'Walford's Gibbet'.

Ann Rice gave birth to Walford's daughter in November 1789, and named her Sarah. Within three months the young mother was dead.

Almost two centuries later, the site was associated with another murder. In 1988 the remains of a young Bristol woman, Shirley Banks, were located at Dead Woman's Ditch. They had been placed there by John David Guise Cannan, the man later found guilty of killing her in Leigh Woods near Bristol. In 2001 the same area was extensively searched in the hope of finding the body of Suzy Lamplugh, an estate agent missing since 1986 and now presumed dead. That search was not successful and Suzy remains officially missing.

3

'I AM ENTIRELY INNOCENT'

Buckland St Mary, 1823

On Thursday 20 February 1823, 13-year-old Betty Trump set out on a journey from which she never returned. She had been living with her grandparents at Buckland St Mary for a year, and within the last fortnight, her mother, Elizabeth, and father, Samuel, had moved to the village to join her. Betty had been asked to go and visit her older sister, Sarah, who had remained in Winsham when the rest of the family moved, to see if she could live with her.

It was a fine morning when Betty began to walk the eight miles to Winsham. She took the turnpike road from Taunton to Chard to the crossroads with the Ilminster to Honiton road, continued through Street Ash to Combe St Nicholas, then Chard and finally Winsham. On her return through Chard she bought some plates, needles and thread, and a pap spoon, before continuing her homeward journey. When she had not reached Buckland St Mary by nightfall, her parents were not unduly worried. A 16 mile walk was a long one for a 13-year-old to make in one day. However, as she had not returned by Saturday morning, they sent her sister, Ann to Winsham, and were horrified to learn on her return that Betty had left Sarah's house by mid-afternoon on Thursday.

Samuel and Elizabeth immediately retraced Betty's footsteps. Before darkness forced them to abandon the search for their daughter, they discovered that she had done her shopping in Chard and had later been seen walking through Combe St Nicholas on her way home. A search party was organised, and as dawn broke, Samuel and a number of friends and relatives began to comb the area for any sign of Betty. At about 7 a.m., her body was found in a wooded area known as Coppice Burrows, about 50yds from the Taunton to Chard road. Her throat had been viciously cut, yet her body seemed unusually peaceful. There were no signs of a struggle, her clothing was undisturbed and her shopping basket was neatly placed beside her, its contents untouched.

Her body was taken to her father's house and examined by John Wheadon, a surgeon from Chard. Although unsure whether Betty had been sexually molested or not, Wheadon said that her throat had been cut with a sharp instrument, such as a knife or a billhook, and that more than one person could have carried out the attack.

Witnesses established a timetable of Betty's movements on the day of her murder. Sarah Trump said that her sister had left Winsham well before 3 p.m.

The grave of Betty Trump, Church of St Mary, Buckland St Mary. (© Nicola Sly)

and had arrived at the shop in Chard, owned by Mrs Mary Rio, about quarter of an hour later. Mrs Rio was able to be precise about the timing as she recalled seeing the mail coach passing while Betty was browsing in her shop. Some thirty minutes later, Betty was buying plates in Mr Treasure's shop, and then she was seen by other witnesses walking through Combe St Nicholas, later going up Stooper's Hill, near Buckland St Mary. A labourer passed her as she walked down the other side of the hill at about 5.30 p.m., then two more witnesses, a couple of labourers, saw her at 5.45 p.m. near Combe Beacon. They were questioned extensively about their possible involvement in Betty's death, but were released without charge. Rumour had it that two or three strangers dressed in sailors' uniforms had been seen near Coppice Burrows at around the time of the murder, but because of the delay in searching for and finding Betty, it was impossible to confirm or deny these rumours.

Betty was to be buried on the following Sunday, but so many people wished to view her body that the funeral was deferred for another week in order to accommodate them. In all, more than 1,500 people came to look, and her coffin lid was screwed down, unscrewed and then screwed down again over and over.

The inquest opened on 25 February. One of the first to give evidence was William Flood, a 26-year-old farm labourer who lived and worked at New House Farm, Buckland St Mary. As her Sunday school teacher since her arrival in the village, he knew Betty well. He recalled hearing cries for help coming from Coppice Burrows on either the previous Thursday or Friday afternoon. Assuming that they came from a child who was being physically chastised at a nearby cottage, he had not gone to investigate as he did not wish to interfere. When asked why he had not mentioned this before, Flood maintained that he did not consider it to be his business, and besides, he had mentioned it to his employer Mr Wyatt soon after the murder had been discovered. The coroner was evidently not satisfied with this reply.

The inquest delivered a verdict of murder by person or persons unknown, but the coroner's remarks to Flood about his failure to assist a person in danger added fuel to the fires of the gossips who were already speculating that he might be guilty. It was rumoured that Betty Trump had pleaded with her mother to be excused from Sunday school and that Flood had been taking 'indecent liberties' with her for some time. There were also allegations that Flood had returned home late on Thursday evening and was reluctant to explain why. Furthermore, there was talk of bloodstained clothes being burned to destroy evidence.

These rumours reached the ears of local magistrate, the Revd Dr Palmer, who promptly issued a warrant for Flood's arrest in connection with the murder. The local constable, Joseph Salisbury, was sent to apprehend Flood and to search his room. His working smock was found with a few spots of dried blood, but these were explained by the fact that he had helped to kill a pig that morning. A bloodstained billhook was also found nearby, but one of the other farm workers, James Vickery, admitted to using it recently to remove the horns from a dead sheep. No other incriminating evidence was found.

Palmer interviewed Flood on the following morning. He was satisfied that the allegations against the suspect were unfounded and he promptly released him, to the immense dissatisfaction of many local people. Palmer then formed a committee to make enquiries into the murder, and one of their first decisions was to offer a reward of £100 for any information relating to the killing. They also obtained approval from the Home Secretary, Sir Robert Peel, to offer an amnesty from prosecution for anyone who was involved in the murder but had not actually committed it. Finally, they engaged a Bow Street Runner, Samuel Taunton, to investigate the killing.

Several local men were questioned, but Flood remained the chief suspect and was eventually arrested by Taunton on 8 March. He was brought before local magistrates who remanded him in custody pending further questioning. Asked to account for his movements on the day of the murder, he said that he had been muck spreading. He denied all rumours that he had been hedge laying, using a billhook, and two witnesses who had seen him at work in the fields backed up his recollections. Flood admitted to having seen Betty pass the field in which he had been working on her way to Chard, but maintained that he had not seen her again. At around 5.30 p.m. he had broken off from muck spreading to feed the cattle, and then walked home to New House Farm, arriving at about 6.15 p.m. On his way home he had met a lady named Honor Marsh near the crossroads and shortly afterwards, had heard cries coming from cottages towards Buckland Hill.

Taunton searched Flood's room again and found a small knife. The shirt that Flood had worn on the day of the murder was also retrieved and found to bear no bloodstains. Flood engaged the services of a local lawyer, Mr Cox, to defend him but Cox was obstructed by both the magistrates and the committee and was thus unable to see his client until 28 March, the date of the first public hearing of the case.

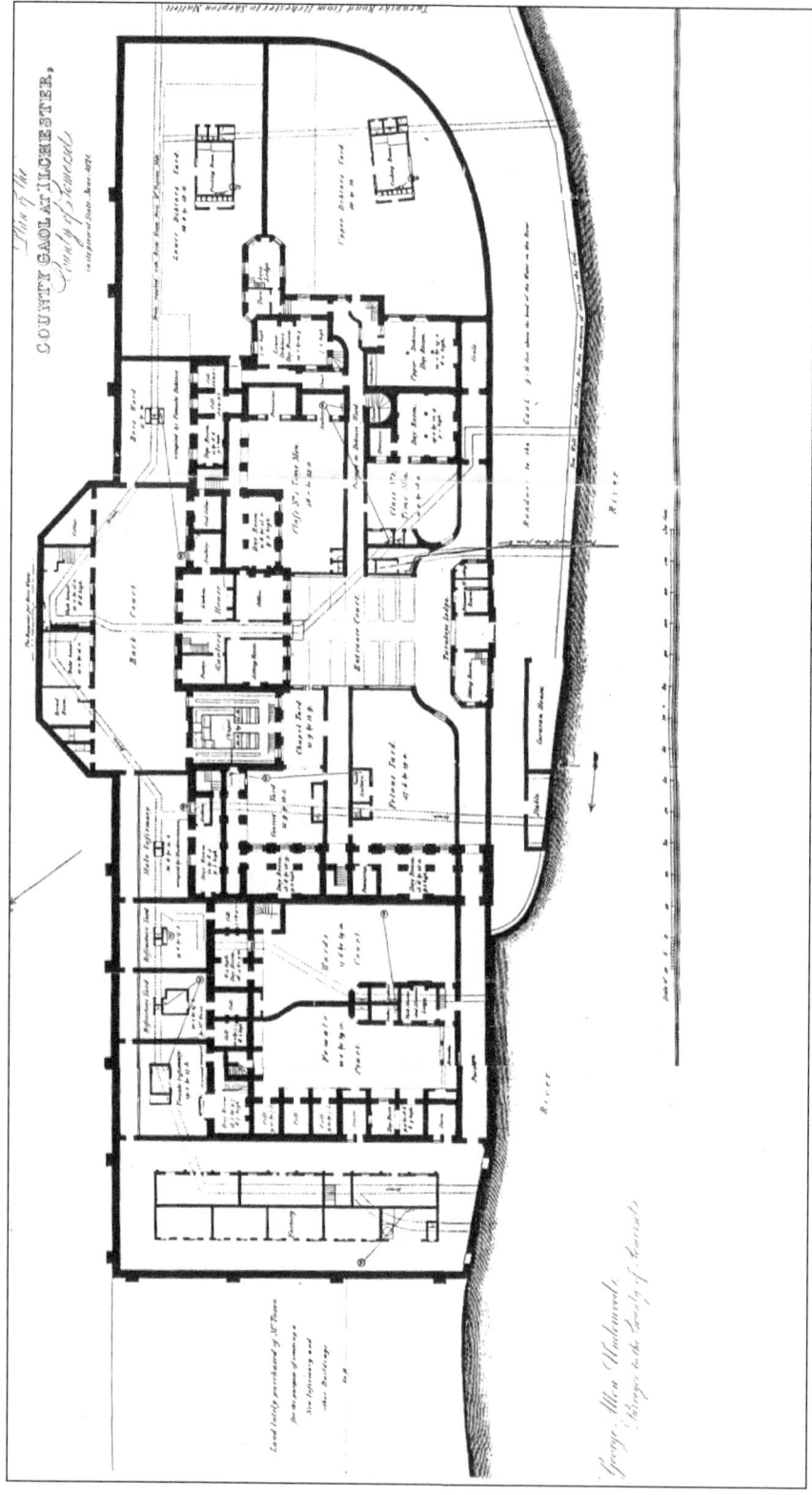

Plan of the County Gaol at Ilchester from 1822.

Meanwhile, the committee went to extraordinary lengths to prove Flood guilty of the murder. Firstly, Philip Wyatt, described as a 'carpenter, poet and soothsayer', was taken to Flood's cell where he maintained that he had spent three nights lying on Betty Trump's grave. On the third night, the dead girl's spirit had appeared and escorted him to the place where the murder had been committed. Wyatt confronted Flood with the news that the spirit had named him as the killer.

The committee also practised 'trial by Bible'. An open Bible was placed outside Flood's room and the front door key of the inquirer's home was laid on the sixteenth verse of the first chapter of the Book of Ruth. This verse reads, 'And Ruth said entreat me not to leave thee or to return from following after thee: for whither thou goest, I will go and where thou lodgest, I will lodge: thy people shall be my people and thy God, my God.' The book was then closed and tightly bound, with part of the key protruding from between its pages. The key was then held between the forefingers of two people who asked, 'Did William Flood commit the murder?' after which the verse was repeated. If the Bible turned fully around before the end of the verse, William was judged to be guilty.

Flood was also visited by one of the committee members, Sir William Templer Pole. He informed Flood that the evidence against him had already been heard at Exeter Assizes and was deemed sufficient to warrant his execution. In spite of these tactics, Flood would not confess to the murder.

The trial opened on 28 March. Samuel and Elizabeth Trump testified that their daughter had never made any allegations of improper conduct against the defendant, nor had she been reluctant to attend Sunday school. They stated that she had not attended on the Sunday before her murder because her two young cousins had visited and she had stayed at home to play with them.

Examination of the witnesses was then adjourned until 7 April. When proceedings resumed, Honor Marsh said she had met William Flood on the road shortly after 6 p.m. on the day of the murder and exchanged greetings with him. However, doubt was cast upon her testimony by blacksmith John Dommett and his apprentice, Samuel Partridge. They gave a detailed account of their work on the day of the murder, which implied that William Flood had passed the smithy at about 7 p.m. This information was seized by the magistrates who felt it disproved Flood's statement that he had been at home at New House Farm by 6.15 p.m., thus giving him enough time to have committed the murder. Mr Cox was not permitted to cross-examine the blacksmith and his apprentice. Had he been allowed to do so, he would doubtlessly have established that the clock by which the blacksmith told the time was usually between thirty and forty-five minutes fast.

Cox later offered to call seven witnesses who would be prepared to swear to the fact that Flood was at New House Farm by 6.20 p.m. on the evening of the murder. The magistrates declined his offer, stating that the evidence already heard had proved that Flood had passed the blacksmith's shop at 7 p.m. and it was not their place to judge between conflicting evidence. At this, Flood protested that he had been promised that his witnesses would be heard, but he was ignored and the magistrates committed him to trial at the Summer Assizes, charged with the murder and violation of Betty Trump. He was taken to Ilchester Gaol to await trial.

The trial opened on 11 August and was presided over by Sir James Burrough. He advised the jury that he believed that the evidence presented at the magistrates' court was insufficient to convict William Flood, who was thereby released. Desperate to clear his name, Flood went straight to the magistrates to try and convince them of his innocence. Magistrate William Hanning commented that too many things were unexplained, and advised him to go and live in America. Nevertheless, Flood returned to Buckland St Mary where he redoubled his efforts to prove his innocence by publishing a small book, outlining the facts of the murder and the content of the depositions put before the magistrates. He included the evidence that would have been presented in court had his witnesses been permitted to testify and also included details of strangers seen near the murder site around the time of the killing. Within the book were several certificates signed by residents of Buckland St Mary supporting Flood's declaration of innocence.

Drawing of William Bridle, gaoler at Ilchester 1808–21, by George Cruikshank.

The murder of Betty Trump was never solved, and it seems that there were never any real suspects, apart from Flood. Some twelve years later, his name was again brought to public attention, following the publication of a letter written by William Norman, a surgeon, in *The Sherborne Journal* on 24 August 1835. Norman had been called to attend Flood, who was suffering from chronic heart disease, and having broken the news to him that he was dying, was asked by Flood to draw up a statement and issue it on his behalf. He then dictated and signed the following statement:

> I, William Flood believing that my end is fast approaching and that I shall shortly appear before Him from whom no secrets are hid, declare solemnly, and as it were my dying breath, that I am entirely innocent of the foul charge of murder, of which I have been accused, and I know nothing whatever relating to the commission or contemplation of the dreadful deed.

The declaration, dated 22 August 1835, was signed by William Flood and witnessed by William Norman, surgeon. He survived only hours after making his statement, allegedly still protesting his innocence until his very last breath.

4

'THERE ARE THIEVES IN THE HOUSE!'

Bath, 1828

In the autumn of 1826, Richard Gillham came to work as a butler for Mrs Coxe, a reasonably wealthy widow at 16 Marlborough Buildings, Bath. Aged 23, a native of Taplow, Buckinghamshire, Gillham had previously held a similar position with the Revd Vansittart Neil. After working for Mrs Coxe for about a year, he married the cook. Neither the cook's first name nor her age have been traced, but as she had been employed there for about eleven years, it can be assumed that she was several years older, and it is possible that he may have married her more for her money than for anything else. More to the point, he probably had an eye on somebody else's money as well, as Mrs Gillham hoped for an annuity from the elderly Mrs Coxe after her death.

Mr Gillham was not too proud to steal, as one of the other servants, Maria Bagnall, soon found out. An honest, high-principled young woman aged about 25, she resented this dishonesty on the part of a fellow-employee, and informed Mrs Coxe. The latter was evidently unaware that her butler and her cook had recently become husband and wife, for she was probably one of those who did not look too well on two of her servants getting married. At any rate, sometime around late 1825 or early 1826, she decided that Mr and Mrs Gillham would have to go, and gave them notice to leave. Richard had overheard conversations between Mrs Coxe and Maria Bagnall, and he knew who was responsible for their plight.

The front attic of the house at Marlborough Buildings was a large room, divided by a communicating door. Mr and Mrs Gillham slept on one side and Maria Bagnall on the other. At around 2 a.m. on Sunday 27 January 1828, Gillham claimed he was awakened by a noise which sounded like somebody boring a hole through the door. Suspecting burglars, he went to the door at the bottom of the attic stairs. Nearby was a closet where the plate chest and other valuables were kept, and here he noticed an intruder picking the door lock. He crept back to the bedroom, loaded three pistols, and returned downstairs. When he tried to raise the latch and open the door, he found it had just been fastened. Suspecting that the burglar was on the other side, and pushing it shut, he discharged one pistol, taking aim in the direction which he thought would give him the greatest chance of hitting the person. The shot went through the door and struck against the wall on the opposite side of the landing. Gillham then ran to the window of the back of the attic, firing another shot, then to the opposite window at the front, shooting a third time, shouting out 'Murder! Murder!'

By this time, watchmen were coming towards the house. They knocked at the front door and Gillham called out, 'For God's sake run round the field-side, for there are thieves in the house, and I am fastened in!' Three watchmen entered and came upstairs, calling to the rest of the household. As one came upstairs, Gillham burst a door open. It normally was shut with a latch outside, and the thieves had driven a gimlet into the lintel of the door just above the latch, which had prevented him from opening it. Once he had got free, he went downstairs with the watchmen.

One patrolman, James Dawkins, who had been drawn towards the house by the sound of the pistols, discovered the dead body of Maria Bagnall on the floor of the upper kitchen, covered with blood. A large club lay beside her.

Mr King, the surgeon, arrived at the house about 2.45 a.m. He was the first to inspect the body of the victim, and found that she had received a severe blow on the head, which had probably rendered her unconscious. She had then been hit over the right eye, the brow of which was much lacerated, and the eye sunk into its socket. The cause of death, which would have been instantaneous, was her throat being cut; the wound extended to the spine, and the head was nearly severed from the body. Her right hand was also much bruised, presumably in an attempt to ward off the blow to her head; and the thumb and middle finger of that hand were much lacerated, the middle finger nearly severed, King assumed, when she had tried to seize the knife. When he had arrived at the house, the body was quite stiff, and the blood around it in a state of coagulation. He thought the murder had been committed about three hours previously, not long before midnight, and the wound in the throat must have caused instant death.

The Royal Crescent, Bath, 1920s.

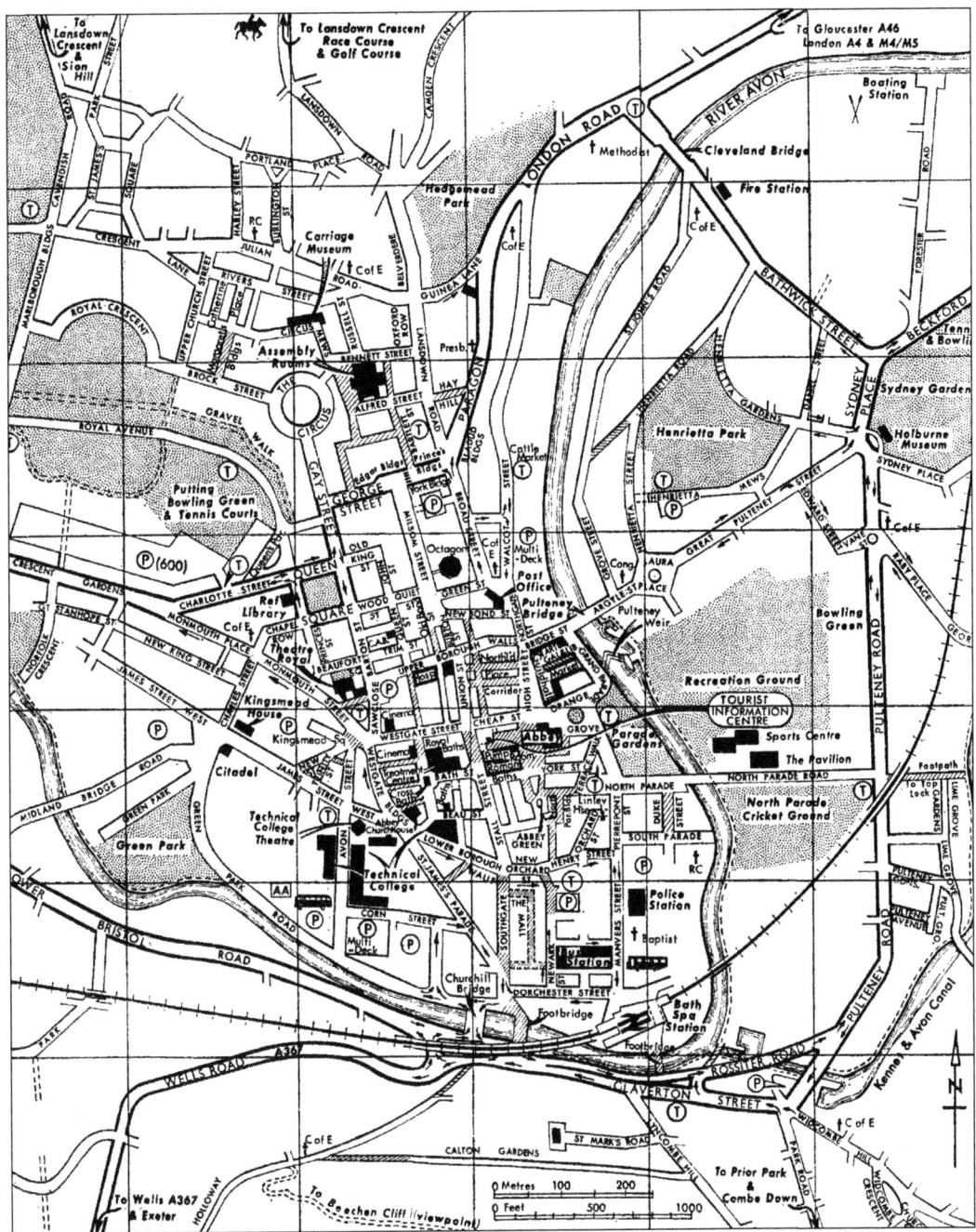

Street plan of Bath.

Pultney Street, Bath.

Several boxes and drawers in the drawing rooms and parlours had been picked and rifled of their contents. A cellaret containing three bottles of wine and a bottle of gin had been broken open. Other items were found near the kitchen door, including a silver tea urn in a case, a bundle containing a pelisse belonging to Mrs Gillham, and Gillham's own greatcoat. On the stairs approaching the attic door a knife was found, but with no signs of blood on it.

An inquest was held later that week at the Guildhall, Bath, with the mayor, G.H. Tugwell, presiding as coroner, and a jury of twenty-one. Richard Gillham said that at about 11 p.m. on Saturday 26 January, he and his wife went to bed. On their way upstairs, they met Maria Bagnall and wished her goodnight. She then went downstairs into the kitchen, as she often did, after the rest of the household had gone to bed, for some water to wash her feet. There was also an elderly womanservant going upstairs at the same time.

After everyone else had been interviewed, that evening, the jury returned a verdict of wilful murder against some person or persons unknown. The churchwardens and overseers of the parish of Walcot, where the murder was committed, offered a reward of 50 guineas for discovery of the offender, and a reward of £100 was offered by the city corporation.

Until then, it had been assumed that Maria Bagnall must have disturbed the burglar or burglars, who killed her in order to escape detection, and that Mr Gillham had come close to discovering them in the act. However, the household, the mayor and the jury felt that Gillham's account of the proceedings did not ring true. Moreover, it was known that he bore Maria Bagnall a grudge. Was he exacting his revenge on her for the imminent dismissal of his wife and himself? He was arrested on suspicion of murder, and he and his wife were examined by Tugwell and Mr Bourne, the prison keeper.

When the latter spoke to Mrs Gillham on her own, she told him that when her husband had returned upstairs to bed on the night of the murder, he seemed strangely ill-at-ease. When she asked him if something was wrong he refused to tell her, merely ordering her 'not to say a word to Nanny [an elderly fellow-servant] about his going down stairs'. If anybody was to ask her she must say that he had not gone downstairs at all, and that he had gone to bed before she did.

It became clear that any 'robbery' on the premises had been faked, especially after a large quantity of goods was found in Gillham's private lodgings. He had ample reason for wanting Maria Bagnall out of the way, by fair means or foul. When he left the room where he had been questioned, he exclaimed to everyone present, 'Well, I know they'll hang me for this, but thank God, I am innocent of the murder!' 'Don't say a word about it – don't add lies to crime!' Mr Bourne cautioned him. Gillham shrugged his shoulders; 'Ah! We [he and his wife] have been like bees during the last summer, collecting our honey; and now, like bees, I suppose our hive will be destroyed and our honey taken.' He knew when he was beaten.

Early on Sunday 3 February he was taken to Shepton Mallet Gaol to await trial at Taunton Assizes on 27 March. He admitted his crime, and was sentenced to death. In May his wife gave birth to a child, and this was the one consolation for her sufferings, as she wrote to her husband in prison that she was 'neglected and looked cold upon by every person whom she had formerly been friendly with, and that suspicions were entertained that she was privy to the committal of the crime, and that her life was embittered for ever.' He declared that his wife was innocent; he alone was responsible, and he wished he had told her beforehand of his intention to kill, for then she would have talked him out of it. To his friends at Taplow, he wrote that he fully deserved his punishment and begged them not to grieve for him, 'for I am not worthy for you to trouble about, for my sufferings are not half bad enough for me – they are nothing compared to my sins, which are great…oh! What could have possessed my worldly heart?'

He was hanged at Ilchester Gaol on 4 June 1828. Describing the scene, the *Taunton Courier* said that he 'had no appearance that bespoke the ruffian, but looked a respectable servant man; and had rather a mild look than otherwise.'

Shortly after the trial, the Revd W. Downes Willis, curate of the Holy Trinity Church at Bath, preached a series of sermons on the subject of dishonesty on the part of domestic servants, which he saw as all too prevalent. These did not go down well with local manservants. He was mobbed in the streets afterwards by some who thought he had brought disgrace on their profession, and a hare's skin filled with fat was tied to the knocker of his front door. Although warned that his next sermon was liable to interruption, he refused to be deflected, and took as his text a line from Galatians 4:16: 'Am I therefore become your enemy, because I tell you the truth?' The congregation respectfully heard him out, rose as one and quietly left at the end.

5

'NOT A FORTNIGHT LONGER! MARK MY WORDS'

Withypool, 1829

The noise of spirited arguments filtering through the walls of her cottage in the remote Exmoor village of Withypool on the evening of Sunday 5 July 1829 no longer fazed Mrs Ann Quick. Although her neighbours, Abraham and Mary Reed had been married for only a year, Mrs Quick had become used to their frequent rows, often accompanied by the sounds of crockery smashing. Besides, it was soon apparent that today's row was finished, and she could look forward to peace and quiet. However, it would not last. Half an hour later she heard Reed calling for her assistance, as his wife had been taken ill. Mrs Quick rushed next door where she found Mary being supported in a chair by her husband, apparently in the throes of a fit which lasted about ten minutes. According to Abraham Reed, such fits were all too common. Gradually Mary's spasms ceased and she seemed to regain her senses, asking for a cup of tea. Reed made her one, and after she had drunk it, she appeared to be better.

Ann Quick returned to her cottage, but later that day heard Abraham Reed calling for help again. This time she found Mary vomiting violently, complaining loudly that she had been poisoned and was about to die. Ann tried to comfort the distraught woman, asking her why she thought that she had been poisoned. Mary replied that she had breakfasted on bread spread with some cream that her husband had brought her, and that he had put arsenic in it. Reed had disposed of the remainder of the cream by tipping it into a mud pond outside their home. He had also broken the cup containing the cream and thrown it away. He claimed to have eaten some of the cream as well at Knighton Farm, where he was occasionally employed, before bringing the rest home for his wife. He ridiculed Mary's assertions, saying she was always complaining that things he brought home were dirty or poisoned.

Quick suggested to Reed that a doctor should be called, but at this, Mary became almost hysterical, saying she would be dead before the doctor could get there. Hence no medical opinion was sought on Mary's condition, which appeared to worsen considerably during the evening. She was now complaining of severe pain in her stomach, in addition to the frequent, violent vomiting. Her husband disposed of the vomit by throwing it into the mud pond outside.

Withypool, 1950s.

Ann Quick returned home for the night, going back to her neighbours' house on the following morning. There she found Mary in bed, still suffering agonising stomach pains. Mary pleaded with Ann to summon the Revd Mr Boyce, the local clergyman, to come and bleed her, and Ann went to fetch him. On her return, she was met by a sobbing Abraham, who told her that Mary had died. She was 30 years old.

The village undertaker and carpenter, John Thorne, was asked to supply a coffin. By this time, rumour was rife in the small village and Thorne suggested that, to allay the gossip, Reed should have his wife's body examined by Mr Collyns, a surgeon from Dulverton. A reluctant Reed was persuaded to borrow a horse and set out to consult the surgeon. On his return, he told Thorne that Collyns would be coming to examine the body tomorrow. Reed expressed his concerns that the surgeon might want to open the body, wondering how he might prevent this from being done. Mary, he told Thorne, had expressed a strong revulsion for such examinations and would surely haunt anyone who tried to open her body for as long as they might live.

In the event, Collyns did open the body, finding the dead woman's intestines to be very inflamed. He removed these organs and sealed them in a bottle, taking them away for more detailed examination. Before he left the house, he was informed that a pig belonging to the Quick family had also died that morning. Collyns decided to examine the dead pig too and found that the animal also had highly inflamed intestines. He removed these, sealing them in a second bottle.

A closer examination of both sets of internal organs, which included tests for arsenic and other corrosive substances, revealed no trace of any poison. Yet, no known natural disease could readily explain both the symptoms suffered by Mary and the subsequent death of the pig with similar symptoms. Accordingly, Collyns requested a second opinion from a colleague, Mr Hugh Standert, who re-tested both sets of internal organs, but could find no trace of any poison in either Mary Reed's organs or those of the pig.

Though none of the medical tests had managed to reveal any trace of poisoning, Reed was arrested for the murder of his wife Mary, when police discovered that he had taken out the equivalent of life insurance on his wife and, on her death, stood to receive the princely sum of £6 5s 6d. To add weight to the evidence that prompted Reed's arrest, two shopkeepers came forward to state that he had attempted to buy poison from them only a week before his wife's death.

Reed's trial opened on Friday 27 August 1829 at the Somerset Lammas Assizes at Bridgwater, with Reed proclaiming his innocence of the murder of his wife.

For the prosecution, Mr Erle told the jury that Reed had joined a benefit society at North Molton and that, after being a member for two years, he was entitled to receive a sum of money in the event of his wife's death. Mary Reed had been taken ill shortly after the culmination of the two-year period, having eaten some cream for her breakfast. Robert Stoneman, also a member of the benefit club, testified that Reed had actually speculated beforehand on how much money he would receive, should his wife happen to die. Reed had thrown both the remnants of the cream and his wife's vomit into a mud pond, in which his hens and his neighbour's pigs roamed freely in search of food. Within a short time, one of the pigs and three of the hens had also died, all having shown very similar symptoms to those experienced by Mary Reed.

The two shopkeepers from North Molton, Catherine Burgess and Henry Westcott, testified to the defendant's requests for poison on 29 June. Reed had first approached Burgess, asking for arsenic or mercury, and when told that she did not sell either, had asked if she sold Spanish flies. When told that she did not sell poisons of any kind, he had asked where he might obtain some and Burgess had directed him to the village tailor, John Westcott, who sold groceries and medicines. Watched by his son Henry, Westcott had made up a 3oz packet of arsenic for which he charged Reed sixpence, warning him at the time to take care of it. (He was admonished in court by the Lord Chief Justice for selling arsenic to a stranger and told in no uncertain terms never to do it again.)

Joan Hole, the mother of the farmer who employed Reed on occasions, stated that Reed had asked her if she could spare some cream. She had put ¼lb of scalded cream into a clean cup, which Reed had bought with him. Her entire family had eaten the remaining cream with whortleberry pie, without any ill effects.

Ann Quick testified about being called by Reed to help his sick wife and also told the court that her previously perfectly healthy pig had died shortly after Mrs Reed, as had three of the defendant's fowls. All had access to the mud pond, where Reed had disposed of the vomit and the uneaten remains of the cream.

Collyns and Standert, the two medical men, were next to testify before the court. Collyns related the tests he had performed on the intestines of both Mrs Reed and the pig, and his failure to find any trace of arsenic in either. However, he was able to explain this by suggesting that both Mary Reed and the pig could have purged the arsenic from their systems by vomiting. Collyns also stated that he had asked the defendant directly if he had ever used poison for any purpose, but Reed had denied it, saying that he would not recognise poison if he saw it. At the time, Reed had informed him that his mother-in-law had used poison for baiting rats and that he had seen her mixing it into a mash. Mary Reed sometimes obtained cream from her mother and, Reed stated, she was aware that her mother

Withypool Church. (© Nicola Sly)

kept poison at home. Standert was next to appear on the witness stand and he supported Collyns' findings.

Finally, a witness was called in an attempt to prove that Reed intended to poison his wife. Ann Colmer recalled meeting him about three weeks before Mary's death and having a conversation with him to the effect that he would be going to Winsford Fair on 6 July, if his wife died before then. Colmer had asked why he thought his wife might die, seeing as she had seen her only the previous day and had found her in excellent health. 'Not a fortnight longer! Mark my words' had been Reed's strange reply.

No defence was offered for Abraham Reed, other than his own protestations of innocence, and it took the jury only a few minutes to deliberate the case before returning a verdict of guilty. Asked why he should not be given a death sentence, Reed merely muttered, 'The witnesses have sworn falsely.' He appeared almost in a trance as the sentence was pronounced.

Abraham Reed did not have long to wait before the sentence was carried out. He spent the night in Bridgwater Gaol, and made a full confession of his guilt to the under-sheriff of Somerset on the following morning, admitting that his marriage had not been happy and that he had sought to end it by mixing arsenic with cream, which he then gave to his wife. He was sent to Ilchester Gaol that afternoon and attended Sunday service on the following day, where the subject of the sermon was 'Thou shalt not kill.' The remaining hours of his life were spent with the prison chaplain, who administered the Sacrament to Reed on the Monday morning. At 11.30 a.m. on Monday 30 August 1829, he was shackled and led to the scaffold located outside Ilchester Gaol. In front of a crowd of spectators, he prayed for a short while before the platform beneath his feet dropped, leaving him hanging by the neck. After its removal from the scaffold, his body was given for dissection.

6

'HERE'S A PRETTY BITCH COMING DOWN THE LANE'

Chard, 1829

On the morning of Tuesday 1 December 1829, Harriet White made a shocking discovery as she walked to her workplace at Chard. On a path leading from Lower Touchays to Avishayes Lane, about half a mile from her destination, she almost stumbled over the body of a young woman who had been so badly mutilated that the newspapers of the time reported that she was in 'too horridly mangled a state for the power of language adequately to describe it.' The corpse was cold and stiff, as if she had been lying there all night. Her throat had been slashed, almost separating her head from her body and she had a deep stab wound in one breast that penetrated almost through to her back. Her other breast had been practically severed. Her petticoats were pulled up over her stomach, both her thighs were smeared with blood and a loaf of blood-soaked bread lay beneath her left shoulder.

Harriet White immediately screamed, turned tail and fled, bumping into Jacob and Joan Summers who had been walking the same path a little way behind her. Almost hysterical, Harriet flung her arms around Joan Summer's neck and babbled about her gruesome find. Leaving his wife to comfort White, Jacob Summers hurried on until he reached the body. His first thoughts on seeing the dead woman were to preserve her modesty. He quickly pulled down her petticoats and rearranged her dishevelled clothing before returning to his wife and Harriet.

With the two frightened women left to guard the body, Summers ran to the nearby town of Chard to raise the alarm. Reaching Fore Street, he began to shout 'Murder! Murder! Murder!' at the top of his voice, and was soon joined by several men who came flocking out from their homes and places of work to see what the commotion was about.

Summers led the townsmen back to the murder site, where, after a short discussion between them, he was left to stand guard over the body while the police were summoned from Chard. While Summers was alone with the corpse, he heard the factory bell ring at 8 a.m. As he waited, more and more people arrived in the field, some just passing by on their way to work, others drawn to the scene by morbid curiosity. One arrival was the Chard parish overseer, who swiftly arranged for a cart to convey the body to the workhouse.

A post-mortem examination of the dead woman, carried out by surgeon Northcote Spicer, revealed that she had been repeatedly slashed about the throat, resulting in near decapitation. Both her windpipe and her carotid artery had been severed. Although there were no signs of a sexual assault, a bloody handprint was found on her left thigh and smears of blood on her right. A search of the field in which the body was discovered yielded numerous blood splatters and smears, but no trace of the murder weapon, which, in Spicer's opinion, was a sharp pointed knife. The body was quickly identified and, as soon as a positive identification had been made, police immediately had a likely suspect for her murder.

The deceased woman was 22-year-old Joan Turner who worked in Rist's Lace Factory in Chard and was lodging at nearby Touchays. She was described as being a young woman of the most unimpeachable character, liked and highly respected by her employers and all who knew her. However, there was one person who definitely did not like her. There had long been bad blood between Turner and a fellow worker at the factory, John Russell. Along with another man, Russell had been summoned for the nineteenth century equivalent of what we today would call sexual harassment. He had been brought before magistrates on a charge of 'making work' with Turner, after he had lifted her petticoats. Found guilty as charged, he was fined 5s, thus raising the possibility in people's minds that he had committed the murder in order to get even with Turner.

Chard constables Joseph Salisbury and Robert Norris went straight to Rist's factory and brought 33-year-old Russell back to the workhouse for questioning. Russell, described as 'a decent looking man', accompanied them willingly, denying all knowledge of the murder and readily giving a detailed account of his movements on the previous evening. He had left the factory at 8 p.m., in the company of fellow worker Thomas Harp and gone to Harp's home at Furnham, after which he had picked up some leeks and greens. On his walk home from Harp's house, he had passed several people but had recognised no one in the darkness, although he had wished one man goodnight. By 8.30 p.m., he was eating supper with his wife and infant son. As there was only a small stub of candle in the house, the family had retired to bed early and stayed there until the first ringing of the factory bell the following morning. His wife, Jane, confirmed his story to the last detail.

When questioned by town magistrate, the Revd A.B. Whitehead, he repeated exactly the same story, adding that he had been out drinking with Thomas Harp and his father William on the Saturday prior to the murder. Under the influence of a little too much alcohol, he had slipped and fallen in some mud, and needed to wash his clothes. Both Thomas Harp and his father confirmed that Russell had indeed collected the vegetables on the night of the murder.

Surgeon Spicer was summoned to the workhouse to examine John Russell and noted some small scratches on his face, which he thought might have been made by a child's fingers, possibly in play. He also closely examined the clothing that Russell was wearing at the time and found no bloodstains. Constable Francis Mayo was sent to search Russell's house where he found several items of recently washed clothing. A shirt, waistcoat and a pair of stockings, all of which were still damp, were scrutinised but found to show no traces of blood. No other incriminating evidence was found at the cottage.

Russell was held in custody throughout the inquest into the death of Joan Turner, which lasted for three days before the jury returned a verdict of 'wilful murder against some person or persons unknown'. While in custody, he never deviated from his original statement, and he was released at the conclusion of the inquest as there was judged to be insufficient evidence against him to charge him with the murder.

Yet, even though no formal charge had been made against him, Russell was the brunt of endless gossip and speculation among the people of Chard and, if that was not bad enough, he also had to contend with an ad hoc committee of local businessmen and gentry, formed after the inquest, who were interrogating his workmates, friends and neighbours, seemingly in an effort to tie him to the murder. Russell continued to protest his innocence.

The committee offered a reward of £100 for the discovery of the identity of the murderer, and soon began to collect a great deal of circumstantial evidence against John Russell. It was alleged that a large fire had been observed burning in the kitchen of his cottage in the early morning hours of the night of the murder. Witnesses spoke of hearing the pump in his yard being worked at the same time, and of bloodstained water being seen in the water trough on the following morning. His clothes were damp and it had been noted on his arrival at the factory on the day after the murder that he was unusually clean.

By 21 December, the committee decided that it had assembled sufficient evidence against Russell to warrant his arrest, and he was taken into custody at Ilchester Gaol. With her husband incarcerated, his wife was unable to pay the rent on their cottage and was promptly evicted with her young baby. As Russell was a native of nearby Crewkerne, his family were immediately dispatched to Crewkerne workhouse so that they did not become a financial burden on the parish of Chard. Once they had vacated their cottage, the police moved in for a more thorough search of the premises, this time finding some spots of clotted blood on the staircase and in the bedroom.

John Russell was tried for the murder of Joan Turner at Taunton. The trial opened on Wednesday 7 April 1830, with Russell pleading not guilty. The prosecution was led by Mr Follett, the defence by William Erle. Follett was first to address the court, telling the jury that the majority of the evidence against Russell was circumstantial. He described Joan Turner's last moments, relating how she had left the lace factory at 8 p.m. on 30 November 1829 to walk to her home at Touchays. For part of her journey she had been accompanied by a little girl, 10-year-old Mary Ann Carter, who had spoken of hearing a man jumping over the hedge into the road as the pair walked along together in the dark. Three dreadful screams had been heard at about 9 p.m., coming from the direction of the field where Turner's body was subsequently found on the following morning. Next Follett proceeded to outline the evidence against John Russell – the pump that had been heard working on the night of the murder, the firelight seen coming from his home, the damp clothes, the bloody water, the scratches on his face and the spots of blood found in the cottage after his arrest. He told the jury of the previous quarrel between Russell and Turner, and pointed out that Russell had mentioned the murder to his colleagues before it was officially announced that a body had been found.

Fore Street, Chard, 1920s.

Then Follett called the first of more than seventy witnesses for the prosecution to testify before the court.

Harriet White and Jacob Summers told of the gruesome discovery of the mutilated body. Surgeon Spicer gave the results of his post-mortem and of his examination of John Russell while he was in custody at the workhouse. On cross-examination by Erle for the defence, Spicer again conceded that the blemishes that he had observed on the accused's face looked more like marks from a child's fingernails than scratches and might well have occurred during a play fight.

John Bragg testified to having heard screams at around twenty to nine on the evening of 30 November. Elias England, who had been walking home from Rist's factory with his brother, heard the town clock strike nine as they neared the site of the murder. Just as the clock struck, a man jumped over the hedge and soon afterwards, the boys heard a moaning sound coming from the field where Turner's body was later found. The boys were so startled that they had fled home as fast as their legs could carry them.

Another boy, 12-year-old Robert Bragg, had also been at work at Rist's and had seen John Russell standing by the milestone on the Ilminster Road. Minutes later, Russell had overtaken him.

Next to take the witness stand was 10-year-old Mary Ann Carter, also an employee at the factory. She recalled walking hand in hand with Joan Turner after leaving work at about 8 p.m. After a brief call at a shop, where Joan bought a loaf of bread, the two continued on their homeward journey as far as Stephens Lane, where Mary Ann had heard the man jump over the hedge into the lane. Frightened, she had asked Joan what the sound was and had been reassured by Joan telling her that it was nothing that would hurt her. She and Turner had parted company at Avishayes Lane, after which she had heard no screams or any other sounds. However, she stated that she thought that the man who had jumped over the hedge had been wearing hobnailed boots. Constable Salisbury then told the court that the boots that Russell had been wearing on the night of the murder were hobnailed.

Numerous witnesses followed who testified to the activities at Russell's cottage on the night of the murder, including one, a neighbour, Mary Peedon. She said that she had heard the sounds of a quarrel between two people, and recalled a conversation she had had with John Russell after his release from custody following the inquest in which they had discussed a candle that had been placed in her window. Russell had said that the candle was in place in the window when he arrived home at 8.30 p.m., while Peedon maintained that she had not put the candle there until 9.30 p.m., and her lodger, William Long, thought it had been nearer to 10 p.m. Peedon stated that Russell had then asked her to back him if she was asked to give evidence about the candle, a request that she had promptly refused.

The landlady of the Russells' home, Mrs Clarke, testified that they had taken up tenancy of the cottage in early November 1829 and that she had first observed blood spots on the stairs and in the bedroom in mid-December. Carpenter Thomas Hayball was the final witness to appear on the first day of the trial. He had prepared the cottage for the Russells' occupancy and assured the court that there had been no blood spots anywhere in the house prior to their arrival.

Russell stood in the dock throughout, listening intently to the witnesses, and appearing to be in a state of nervous agitation, struggling to appear composed. Only at 3 p.m. was he allowed a chair.

By a strange twist of fate, the first witness called on the second day of the trial was local builder, Simeon Stuckey, whose brutal murder four months later forms the subject of another chapter in this book. Stuckey presented a model of the Russells' cottage to the court to demonstrate exactly who among his neighbours was able to see their kitchen window. A surveyor followed to say that the place where Turner's body was found was not on her normal route home. This fact was not picked up by the court, but could possibly be significant in that it raises the possibility that Turner may have had a previously arranged assignation.

The next witness to be called was local businessman Benjamin Richards, who had been one of the first people to respond to Jacob Summer's frantic calls of 'Murder!' after the discovery of the body. He had broken the news of the murder to workers from Rist's factory at just after 8 a.m. However, when called before the court, several of Russell's co-workers maintained that Russell had discussed the murder with them well before 8 a.m.

There was much confusion amongst the factory workers about precisely who had said what and when. Some professed to have heard about the murder well before that time, others long after. Some people said that they had heard Russell making threats towards Turner on the day before the murder took place. One, William Guppy, recalled a conversation with Russell as early as March 1829, in which Russell had pointed out Joan Turner as she walked past, saying, 'Look there, here's a pretty bitch coming down the lane,' and announcing his intentions of giving her a 'sly pat' when he got the chance. Another lace worker,

John Atherley, spoke of conversations he had engaged in with Russell before his arrest, in which he alleged that Russell had asked his opinion on whether or not murderers could be saved by repentance. Russell had also supposedly expressed concerns about the powers of a renowned local wizard, conjuror Baker, asking Atherley if he believed that Baker could identify a murderer by second sight.

Finally, several people came forward to act as character witnesses for the accused, amongst them his brother, George. He was able to confirm that the coat, trousers waistcoat and shoes that Russell had been wearing when he was detained on the morning after the murder were the same ones that he had been wearing on the previous day.

After this, Mr Justice Gaselee began to sum up the evidence. He had hardly begun to speak when he was interrupted by one of the members of the jury who said that he need not continue, since they had already made up their minds and were ready to give their verdict. Gaselee informed the jury that it was their sworn duty to listen carefully to the summary and to give it their full deliberation, since this was a complicated case with much room for doubt. In the event, the jury did ask for clarification of the time differences between the prisoner first mentioning the murder in the factory and the event becoming common knowledge. They then deliberated for all of ten minutes, before finding Russell guilty of the murder of Joan Turner.

Before sentence was passed upon him, Russell was asked if he had anything to say. Russell addressed the judge, saying; 'I am free and innocent of the crime, so help me God. I am happy to leave this life and to meet my God under the circumstances I am now placed in.' He then repeated his initial statement, from which he had never deviated throughout the course of his trial, stating that he was 'wholly innocent and know nothing more of the murder than a sucking child and the Almighty will find it out and the world will know that I am innocent!'

Gaselee then pronounced the death sentence on Russell, ordering that he should be executed and his body given to the surgeons for dissection and anatomical research. At this, Russell fell to his knees, protesting; 'My Lord, you have passed sentence of death on an innocent man!'

Scheduled for execution in only a few days, John Russell was taken to Ilchester Gaol to await his fate. However, his defence counsel, William Erle, was not a man to admit defeat so easily and immediately left for Chard to carry out further investigations. Erle was able to secure a temporary stay of execution for his client.

Rumour abounded in the small town of Chard. It was said that Russell had implicated another man from his gaol cell and that, as a result of statements from Russell's wife, two men had been taken into custody. Other gossip suggested that three men had been involved in the murder and similarities were drawn between the death of Joan Turner and that of Betty Trump (see Chapter 3).

Meanwhile, Erle was unearthing some interesting, if disturbing, information about the case. He found that witnesses had been intimidated and interfered with, even to the extent of imprisoning two possible defence witnesses during the trial to prevent them from giving evidence. Much of the evidence against Russell was described as malicious gossip and half-truths and, on 27 April, the day before the rescheduled execution, Erle presented a petition to Robert Peel, the Home Secretary, asking for the King's mercy for his client.

The petition addressed Erle's concerns in great detail, contending that the prosecution had been mistaken about a number of issues including motive, the declarations of the prisoner before the murder and his conduct at the time of the murder, the marks on his face, the evidence surrounding the use of the pump and the bloody water and the blood found in the house. In all, Erle highlighted ten points of concern and the Home Secretary immediately forwarded the petition to Mr Justice Gaselee for investigation.

Meanwhile, Gaselee had been conducting his own investigations into the murder. Immediately after granting the stay of execution, he had instructed three Somerset magistrates, Mr Hobhouse, Mr Phelips and Mr Coombe to make some enquiries in Chard on various matters that had arisen. After considering this new evidence and Erle's petition, Gaselee wrote to Robert Peel stating that, rather than being executed, his recommendation was that Russell should be transported for life.

This apparent about turn did not sit well with the editors of the newspapers of the time, who pointed out that Russell was either innocent of the murder or guilty. If innocent, he should have been discharged, if guilty, he should have been executed; he could not have been moderately guilty of the crime, so should not have been subjected to what they described as a 'half-way action'. It was widely felt that Russell's guilt had been successfully and irrevocably established in court and that he should therefore have been hanged for his crime rather than being permitted to escape the retribution of public justice. In June 1830, John Russell was transported from Ilchester Gaol to Devonport, from where he was transported to Australia for the rest of his natural life.

In *Shocking Somerset Murders*, Jack Sweet relates an anecdote told to him by a descendant of the Russell family. It is alleged that many years after Russell had been transported to Australia, his elderly mother answered the door to a tramp. She recognised the visitor as her son, John, who refused to stay because he was so ashamed of what had happened, but said that he had just wanted to see her again once more before he died.

7

'NEITHER A MURDER NOR A MYSTERY'

Over Stratton, 1830

Simeon Stuckey owned a farm and a building business which in 1830, employed thirty men. On Monday 9 August 1839, some of his workforce were busy building a house in the village of Over Stratton, where Simeon was born and where his parents still lived. It was intended to be a new home for Benjamin Hebditch, a childhood friend of Stuckey's and that afternoon, Simeon decided to ride from his home in Chard to check on the progress of the new building.

At approximately the half-way point of his journey was the Windwhistle Inn, a public house at which Simeon was quite a regular visitor. It had formerly had a reputation for being a haunt of highwaymen, who would lay in wait on the busy London to the Westcountry route, poised to waylay weary travellers. On that hot August evening, it was simply a pleasant place for him to break his journey with a cool pint of cider and a chat with the landlord, Lawrence Biss. He stayed only long enough to quench his thirst before resuming his journey, promising to return on his way home later that night. However, he was not the only drinker in the Windwhistle Inn that afternoon and many of the other patrons could not help but notice that he was carrying a small yellow canvas purse that appeared to be bulging with money.

Simeon arrived at Over Stratton and checked on the building site. From there he went to see Benjamin Hebditch to update him on its progress, leaving Benjamin's house at about 10 p.m. He made a brief call at his parents' home, where his father was ill in bed, apologised for the lateness of the hour and the shortness of his visit, but said that we would visit again soon. He then set off on his return journey to Chard – and was never seen alive again.

At about 11 p.m. a labourer, Robert Perry, heard the sound of a galloping horse pass his cottage, which lay on the route that Simeon Stuckey would probably have taken home. Shortly afterwards, sheriff's officer Mr Norris from Crewkerne found a loose horse on Chillington Common, close to the Windwhistle Inn. Norris decided to lead the horse to the inn to see if the landlord could recognise it and perhaps name its owner. He reached the public house at 1 a.m. and stood in the yard calling for Mr Biss. Roused from his bed, Biss had no difficulty in identifying the horse as Old Tom, the mount of Simeon Stuckey. The horse was still wearing its saddle and bridle and, although cold, was covered in the marks of dried sweat, as though it had recently been heavily ridden. Biss turned the horse

The Windwhistle Inn, Chillington. (© Nicola Sly)

out into his field and the officer agreed to call in on Mrs Stuckey on his return to Chard to let her know the whereabouts of the animal.

At 5.30 a.m. the next morning, Robert Perry set out from his cottage to walk to work. He had not gone far when he spotted what appeared to be a pool of vomit at the side of the road in a field gate. Shortly afterwards, he came across a hat, which he picked up and took back to his cottage, telling his daughter, Amy, to pass it to anyone who enquired about it. Another local resident, Susan Matthews, walked the same stretch of road later in the morning. She too saw the vomit and also what she thought was blood on the road. Near to the pool of blood lay a large stick and the dusty road bore traces of a scuffle and drag marks, as if something heavy had been pulled across the road.

Meanwhile, Old Tom continued to graze peacefully in the field at the Windwhistle Inn. When the horse had not been claimed by teatime, Biss saddled and bridled him and arranged for a boy to ride him back to Stuckey's home in Chard.

That evening, one of Mrs Stuckey's servants appeared at the inn, asking how the horse had come to be kept there overnight. Biss related what he knew about Stuckey's intended movements on the previous day. The servant continued on to Over Stratton and, having made enquiries there and learned that Stuckey had left the village and not been seen since, raised the alarm that all was not well. Search parties, looking for any trace of Stuckey, began the very next morning, but their efforts were fruitless.

As the search continued, rumours began to circulate about Stuckey's fate. In one camp, backed by reporting in the local paper, the *Western Flying Post*, were those who believed that Stuckey had been murdered. However, the rival local paper, the *Taunton Courier*, felt that the builder's disappearance had been deliberately engineered for him to escape his debts. 'The mysterious murder is neither a murder nor a mystery', it claimed, reporting that Stuckey was overdrawn at the bank and questioning the fact that nobody living in the cottage within 10yds of the location of the blood and vomit had heard any sounds of a struggle, even though they had heard a horse passing. The hat and stick had been left in the road as a blind, to lead people to the inevitable conclusion that Stuckey had been attacked on his journey home. The *Courier* also pointed out that Stuckey's businesses had been sold very quickly after his disappearance, stating that this did not augur well for his creditors.

The two newspapers waged an all-out war over what each considered to be the facts of the disappearance. The *Western Flying Post* countered every allegation made in the *Courier*, even offering a reward of £100 for information leading to the capture and conviction of the murderer.

It was the last day of August before the *Post*'s version of events was verified. Two farm workers, Edmund and Charles Harris, were working in a cornfield when they stumbled across a badly decomposed body which had been ravaged by birds and wild animals. Only a notebook in the pocket of the corpse's coat identified it as the body of Simeon Stuckey. The coat was torn as though it had been used to drag the body, and the ground was grooved where Stuckey's spurs had dug small channels into the earth. His gold watch and fob chain were still attached to his waistcoat and his purse, still containing £13 12s 6d, had not been stolen. A post-mortem examination revealed a severe skull fracture, almost six inches in length. In the opinion of the surgeons who conducted the examination, Mr Eustace and Mr Sylvester, this would likely have caused the deceased to vomit, following which death would be almost instantaneous. If Stuckey had vomited, then there was no way that he could have moved from the place where the vomit was found to his present location unless someone had moved him there.

Now that his body had been found, friends rushed to defend Stuckey's reputation and a letter was printed in The *Western Flying Post* refuting the contents of the recent articles printed by the *Taunton Courier*. Of course the businesses had been sold quickly, explained the writer of the letter – how could Stuckey's grieving widow be expected to cope alone with managing a farm and a building business? His account at the bank was overdrawn, by the princely sum of 18s 6d. In fact, the bank owed him money for building work he had done there.

An inquest returned a verdict of murder by person or persons unknown. Suspicion naturally fell on a number of strangers whose presence had been noted in the area on the night of the killing. A Chard man, William Smith, had been returning from a funeral held that afternoon at Chillington Church when he met a stranger whom he described as being medium-sized and wearing a light fustian jacket. Shortly afterwards, Smith met another stranger, who asked whether Smith had seen a man answering the description of the first man he had passed. According to Smith, the enquirer was of very similar build to the first man he had encountered and was wearing identical clothes, clothes that were also similar to the ones Stuckey had been dressed in on the day of his disappearance. Another stranger, a man wearing a dark coat and light trousers and mounted on a horse, had been asking for directions to Chard and had tried to persuade a woman to show him the way. The woman, Margaret Lucy, had felt uncomfortable with the stranger's questions and had fled for her home, bolting the door behind her.

So much time had passed between the murder and the discovery of the body that there was no hope of ever identifying the mysterious strangers. A Bow Street Runner, Samuel Taunton, was brought in to investigate the murder but he was unable to identify the killer or killers, even after the reward money was raised to £500 which, in the 1830s, would have been the equivalent of twenty years wages to a farm labourer.

Several anomalies came to light at Stuckey's inquest. Firstly, there were considerable discrepancies in the times at which various witnesses saw Simeon Stuckey at the Windwhistle Inn. The landlord, Lawrence Biss, stated that Stuckey had arrived at the inn at about 5 p.m. and stayed for only ten minutes. However, another drinker testified that it had been nearer to 6.30 p.m. when Stuckey had arrived. Biss also stated that his wife had been away for the afternoon, arriving home between 8 and 9 p.m., by which time all the inn's customers had left. Yet Hugh Clark, who had spent the evening at the Windwhistle, testified that Mrs Biss had arrived home just as he left, at half past seven.

Then there was the riddle of Stuckey's money. The sum of £13 12s 6d was found in the purse still in Stuckey's pocket when his body was found. Yet, according to his friend, Benjamin Hebditch, Stuckey was carrying around £60 in cash on the day of the murder. Was Hebditch mistaken, or had the money been stolen? Was money the motive for Simeon Stuckey's murder?

Stuckey was buried on 2 September in the graveyard at the Independent Church in Chard where he was a frequent worshipper. The identity of his killer or killers was never determined and his murder remains unsolved.

8

'I CAN'T BEAR TO SEE IT!'

Sandpit Hill, near Langport, 1835

Late in the evening of Friday 6 March 1835, Charles Davis and two young female companions were returning from Curry Rivel to Langport. On their walk back past the Bell Inn, they were passed by a man driving a cart along the road. The man was John Harvey, a well-known local plumber and glazier, who had just been on business in Curry Rivel and had bought himself some cider. As he drew alongside the three people on foot, Davis wished him goodnight and asked whether he could take the women back to Langport. Harvey politely said no, perhaps fearing that giving a lift to two probably inebriated women might have had consequences that could lead to scandal ill-befitting a local businessman of good reputation.

Davis and his friends met another group of people on their way back, stopped to chat, and resumed their journey on foot sometime later. Shortly before midnight, the threesome reached Sandpit Hill, halfway between Curry Rivel and Langport. They were surprised to find Harvey's horse standing across the road and the cart against the bank. At first there was no sign of Harvey himself, but as Davis walked around the horse, he could just make out a dark form lying prostrate on the ground. Assuming this was a drunken Harvey who had fallen out of his cart, Davis tried to rouse him, telling him to get up. There was no response, and Davis assumed that he would need assistance in getting back into the cart. The three youngsters went to seek help at a turnpike cottage quarter of a mile away. They summoned a gatekeeper, who lit a lantern and accompanied them back to Sandpit Hill. There they found Harvey lying on his back, his clothing disordered and his trouser pockets turned inside out. His head had been battered and his lower jaw so badly shattered that his teeth were scattered around. Davis left the gatekeeper to watch over the corpse, and went as quickly as possible to Langport where he raised the alarm at the New Inn and then went on to break the dreadful news to John Harvey's widow.

Harvey's body was taken to the inn. As the coroner, Mr Richard Caines, was away on business, the inquest had to be delayed until the coming Monday. Local magistrates Vincent Stuckey and T.B. Uttermare, with several prominent residents, made a start on trying to hunt down the person or persons responsible and contacted Taunton police officer, Mr Pomeroy.

On Saturday morning they began making enquiries along the road from Curry Rivel to Langport. Mrs Elizabeth Cottle, a wealthy widow who lived in

Portfield House, about 200yds north of the main road, told them that on the Friday evening, she had gone to bed at about 10 p.m. and heard a disturbance about an hour later from the direction of Sandpit Hill. It was a calm night and the sound had carried well on the strong south-westerly wind. Aware that something peculiar was going on, she had asked her servant to open the bedroom window, but by then the noise had stopped. However, soon afterwards she had heard voices in the lane outside her house, followed by the sound of a splash as something was thrown into the nearby pond. As no murder weapon had yet been found, the police arranged to have the pond drained.

Later that day, several men were taken in for questioning. One, John Cothard from Muchelney, a workman employed by Harvey, and another, Samuel Tucker, a labourer from Huish Episcopi, were both released without charge. At around the same time, John Abrahams, another employee of Harvey, who was still shocked by the murder, was in the workshop when John Hoare, one of Harvey's apprentices, came in and asked if a soldering iron he had been using on Friday had been found. Abrahams had been unaware of the missing iron, a development which did not appear significant at the time. Hoare returned on Sunday afternoon and asked again if the iron had come to light. Abrahams asked him whether he had been carrying the iron in the cart with him, and Hoare told him angrily not to bother about it any more. Abrahams began to have his suspicions, which would prove to be all too well-founded. He mentioned it to the police, who decided to have the pond near Portfield House drained that same day. Arthur Stuckey, a local shopkeeper, supervised the operation and was interested when they found a large soldering iron. Though it had been in the water for at least a day, it revealed traces of blood and hair. Hoare was involved in the search, and immediately identified the iron as having belonged to Harvey, a pronouncement which, though truthful enough, would cost him dearly. A medical examination confirmed that the hair was Harvey's as well.

On Monday 9 March, an inquest was opened by Mr Caines at the New Inn. Harvey's body was viewed by a seventeen-strong jury, which then adjourned to the Guildhall and sat until the early evening. That same morning several more men were taken into custody, and two soon emerged as the prime suspects. In the evening, the inquest was adjourned until 10 a.m. the next day. About half an hour after its resumption, one of the magistrates, Vincent Stuckey, entered the room and told everyone that one of the persons being detained was confessing to the murder, and the coroner immediately adjourned the inquest a second time. Coroner and jury reassembled at 10 a.m. the following day, and the Guildhall was packed with spectators as two men were escorted into the room. They were identified as John Hoare and William Howe, two cousins aged 19, and both apprentices to Harvey. They had been taken in for questioning on Monday and quickly confessed to the murder and robbing of the dead man. Hoare had implicated a Mr Nichols in the killing, but this was soon exposed as a lie. They also admitted to stealing four sovereigns, a small diamond and some bills of sale, and told the coroner where these could be found. A sovereign was discovered from under a bedpost in Howe's bedroom and two sovereigns, the diamond and the bills of account were dug up in the garden of Hoare's father; Hoare had already spent the fourth sovereign. When he was lodged at an inn just before he was taken to prison, he looked coldly at the other customers and told them that they 'ought to subscribe around, and treat me with some beer.'

After hearing the confessions, the jury returned a verdict of 'Wilful Murder against John Hoare and William Howe', and the prisoners were committed to Ilchester Gaol to await trial at the Somerset Lent Assizes.

On 3 April 1835 before Mr Justice Pattison, John Hoare was charged with 'having on the 6th of March, feloniously, maliciously, and with malice aforethought, with the right hand striking John Harvey, with a soldering iron, on the left ear, and giving him a mortal wound; and the said William Howe, for aiding and abetting the same.' After hearing supporting evidence from various witnesses, the prisoners' confessions were read to the jury.

A week before the murder, William Howe had been dismissed by John Harvey, who refused to pay him for work carried out before his dismissal. John Hoare agreed that he had been treated unfairly, and between them, they decided that if Harvey did not do the decent thing and pay up, they would have to resort to other methods. When they heard that he was going to Curry Rivel on Friday evening, they planned to lay in wait for him on his return home. The cousins met at the Angel in Langport early that evening, and for Dutch courage, fortified themselves with a pipe of tobacco and two quarts of beer and gin. They then walked to Harvey's house to ask when he was expected back, and his wife told him that he would not be long. She also asked Hoare if he would stay and stable the horse on her husband's return. Hoare excused himself on the grounds that he had to meet someone and then went into the plumber's workshop where he collected his personal tools and also the heavy soldering iron he had used that afternoon. They then went back to Hoare's home where they had supper and, having told his mother that they planned to meet Mr Harvey, set out again.

The plan was simple enough. Howe would grab hold of the horse's head and Hoare would attack Harvey himself. As the latter drew alongside, Hoare called out that he had come to meet him. Harvey asked why, and then asked if his wife would not be angry at his being out so late? Almost at once Hoare threw himself on the man and hit him hard on the head with the soldering iron. Harvey fell forward onto his horse's back and then to the ground. Howe had been holding the animal steady but after turning it across the road, he fled into an adjoining field where he crouched, trembling with fear. Hoare jumped down from the cart, but as he began to turn out his master's pockets, the plumber regained consciousness and called out weakly to him to stop. Hoare responded by battering Harvey with the soldering iron. A horrified Howe begged him to stop, telling him that 'I can't bear to see it!', but Hoare was adamant that he would make sure Harvey would not regain consciousness.

After they had been though their victim's pockets, they ran away across the fields towards Portfield House where Hoare washed the blood from his hands in a ditch and threw the iron into the pond. They shared the meagre proceeds between themselves and then returned to Langport, where Hoare strove to cover his tracks by calling back to Mr Harvey's house to ask if he had returned yet.

The jury wasted little time on such a clear-cut case before returning a guilty verdict. Mr Justice Pattison donned the black cap and told the prisoners that they had been found guilty on the clearest evidence, and on their own confessions, 'of a most foul and atrocious murder'. He told Hoare that:

> There seems to have been no quarrel between you and him, therefore what motive you could have for committing this foul crime, remains in your own breast, whether it was done merely for the purpose of robbing him, or some vengeful motive, you alone and God can tell, for no man but yourself knows; but there is not the slightest doubt, both from the evidence and your own confession that you did strike him on the head with that instrument, and kill him, and that you must have gone out with the sole intention of so doing.

Howe, he said, was as guilty as Hoare. 'There can be no hope of mercy for either of you in this world and it is an offence which human law cannot pass over, neither can those who have the administration of the law in any case of murder, clearly proved, hold out any hopes of mercy. I tell you distinctly and plainly your time is limited in this world to next Monday and I therefore beg and beseech you to make the best possible use of your time in endeavouring to obtain pardon hereafter.' As they were sentenced to hang, Hoare continued to show the same lofty indifference he had evinced during the trial, but the distressed Howe hid his face in a large handkerchief.

At 11 a.m. on 6 April, the prisoners appeared before a large jeering crowd in front of Ilchester Gaol. Howe was clearly affected from the start, and even Hoare's nonchalance collapsed as the rope was put around his neck. It was customary for a man on the scaffold to drop his handkerchief as a signal for the trap to fall, but instead Hoare threw it angrily away from himself with 'insolent obduracy of heart, and died amidst the universal execration of the multitude.'

9

BARE-KNUCKLE FIGHT AT THE RUNNING HORSE

Yeovil, 1843

Bare-knuckle fights were common in the nineteenth century, and there was always an element of risk that for one participant, such a contest could end in something far worse than injury. One such instance occurred during a heavy drinking session at the Running Horse at the appropriately-named Wine Street in Yeovil one Saturday afternoon, 25 March 1843. Having consumed more than was good for him, one of the customers, Henry Philips, kicked over his stool, staggered over to a soldier and challenged him to a fight.

As the soldier rolled his sleeves up, another man, William Crocker, came forward. A huge, heavily-built man and renowned pugilist, he had a reputation to defend. He said loudly that he was the best fighting man in the area, and nobody was going to deny him his title. Another man, Rifleman George Watkins of the Rifle Brigade, then lodging at the Running Horse, proclaimed that he would prove himself better than the lot of them. Crocker immediately accepted the challenge, both men removed their jackets and went into the yard outside, followed by Crocker's wife and a group of other drinkers.

Later, one of the spectators, Robert Anning, a local butcher, would describe the events which followed and how he had watched Crocker and the soldier square up to fight. They traded blows evenly at first and then Crocker landed a hefty punch which sent Watkins crashing against the wall of the yard. As he fell, Watkins's head struck a stone and he slid to the ground, dazed. Quick to take advantage, Crocker bent down, grabbed the front of his opponent's shirt, pulled him to a sitting position and hit him hard across the face. Watkins staggered to his feet, but was then battered to the ground and hit about the head by Mrs Crocker. This was too much for some of the spectators, who shouted 'Unfair, unfair!', and Crocker stood back. Though at a disadvantage, Watkins managed to continue for a while. Two seconds were chosen, Mr Grey for Watkins, and Henry Leach for Crocker. The fight resumed but Watkins, bleeding profusely from his nose, mouth and from cuts around his eyes, was clearly beaten. The police had been alerted, and on arrival, put a stop to the contest.

Alfred Etheredge, who later became Yeovil's first full-time town surveyor, was working in his father's accounts office a few doors away when he heard the commotion from the yard of the Running Horse. As he went to investigate, he found the gate to the yard bolted, but could see the fight as he peered through a crack. After watching for a few minutes, he went back to his work, but the persistent noise was impossible to ignore, and he returned. Although the fight had stopped, people were still milling about in the yard, and Etheredge saw Watkins being helped back indoors. Also disturbed at his duties that day was coach builder John A'Court, who was in a carriage workshop next door to the Running Horse. When the noise started, he looked over the wall to see what was going on. He would later describe the unequal contest and how the soldier had been badly beaten.

The severely wounded Watkins was taken into the kitchen of the inn, where Crocker continued to attack him, even though he was in no state to respond. After Crocker was persuaded to stop, Watkins was given some cider, but it made him very sick, and he was then put to bed.

In spite of his injuries, he was soon well enough to get up. On 29 March, four days after the fight, he came out of the inn and met a local surgeon, Arnold Coles, in Wine Street. He told the surgeon that he had been unwell for the last few days with a persistent headache. Coles looked at him, and particularly the bruising about his eyes and forehead, and then asked what he had been doing. Watkins said he had been walking beside the River Yeo and had slipped down the bank, hitting his head as he fell into the water. As he was shivering and feverish, the surgeon took him back into the inn, bled him, gave him some medicine and had him sent back to bed. The next day he visited Watkins again and thought he seemed to be improving. However, he began to deteriorate during the following week. Realising the truth could be concealed no longer, the landlady told Coles about the fight. When the surgeon asked why he was not told before, a crestfallen Watkins said he thought that Mr Coles would consider it disgraceful behaviour. By now it was too late, and despite all the surgeon could do, Watkins died at 4 a.m. on 12 April.

In a post-mortem carried out by Coles and another surgeon, Mr William Shorland, it was concluded that death had been caused by congestion of the brain and its blood vessels resulting from blows to the head, aggravated by exposure to cold. An inquest was held by the coroner, Mr Caines, in the Moon Inn on Good Friday, 15 April. The jury viewed the body of George Watkins which lay in the Running Horse, and it was reported that the deceased was 'a very fine-grown good-looking man' but who presented a 'sad spectacle from the injuries received in a fight.'

Robert Anning, Alfred Etheredge and John A'Court were summoned as witnesses. They all testified that the fight had been grossly unfair. After the evidence of Mr Coles, that death had resulted from the blows to the head, the jury returned a verdict of manslaughter against William Crocker. The coroner issued a warrant for the arrest of Crocker who had fled the town following Watkins's death, and he was arrested in Crewkerne a few days later.

He was brought before Mr Justice Coleridge at the Somerset Lammas Assizes in Bridgwater at 9 a.m. on Saturday 12 August 1843 and. indicted for feloniously killing George Watkins by striking and beating and throwing him to the ground. A second charge was added indicting Crocker for common assault. Prosecuting counsel was Mr Fitzherbert and Mr Kinglake defended the prisoner.

Mr Fitzherbert opened by recounting the events of 25 March and concluded by declaring that Watkins had died following the ferocious conduct of the prisoner. Alfred Etheredge and John A'Court repeated the evidence they had given at the inquest. The third witness, Robert Anning, told how he had watched the fight from start to finish and added that both men had been drinking heavily beforehand.

Mr Coles then explained the treatment he had given Watkins during the last few days and gave details of the post-mortem examination. He confirmed his opinion, given at the inquest, that death was the result of 'affection of the head caused by blows.' Counsel for the prisoner asked whether the ducking in the River Yeo might have contributed to the 'affection of the head' and Mr Coles agreed that being immersed in very cold water could cause similar appearances in the brain – though it was uncertain whether such immersion had taken place. Re-examined by the prosecution, Coles stated that he had observed the marks of blows about the deceased's eyes and face but none on the head. In reply to a question from Mr Justice Coleridge, the surgeon confirmed that injuries to the face and the appearance of the brain were what he would expect to see after a hard fight with blows struck and with death following.

Mr Kinglake then told the jury that this was a very serious case. No man should consider it without a proper feeling of regret at the unfortunate end of the life of the deceased. Mr Kinglake certainly hoped that nobody who had heard the case would feel it so deeply as the prisoner at the bar. However, the jury should not conclude that the prisoner had been the cause of Watkins's death unless the evidence perfectly satisfied them that he had. Counsel thought that the statement of his learned friend that the prisoner was guilty of ferocious conduct had not been exactly proved but, on the contrary, had it not been for the challenge of the deceased, there would have been no fight. The prisoner at the bar was a peaceable man, he had prevented one fight, and it was only because he had said that he was the best man in the town and would allow no fighting that he had received the challenge. The fight which ensued was one of those common public house quarrels which were best avoided, but which everyone knew regularly took place. Blows were struck on both sides; both men had knocked each other down; and the deceased had received blows about the eyes and forehead which had caused some bleeding, but this was hardly surprising.

There was no evidence that one single blow had killed Watkins. He had also been struck by the prisoner's wife and the soldier, and the prisoner could not be answerable for these blows. The surgeon had told them that he had examined the brain and found inflammation which he had stated was the cause of death. However, he had agreed that no matter how the inflammation had been brought about, it would have proved fatal. Therefore, if the deceased had fallen into the river and got wet and very cold, this could also have accounted for the inflammation.

Mr Kinglake announced that he would prove that a few days before the fight, the deceased had fallen into the River Yeo and afterwards seemed very ill. Because the surgeon had testified that cold could have been a cause of death, he believed the jury might well decide that Watkins had not died as a result of violence at the hands of Crocker.

Next to give evidence was William Dawe of Misterton who said that on the Thursday before 25 March, he had been walking with George Watkins along the bank of the Yeo near Compton Mill, and they were looking for a place to jump across. They eventually found one but when the soldier jumped, he landed heavily and rolled down the bank into the freezing river where he remained for some time trying to get out. When he finally succeeded, he was exhausted, shivering and evidently unwell.

In summing up, Mr Justice Coleridge stated that if in a fair fight, one man struck another and killed him, he would be guilty of manslaughter. The jury had heard from the surgeon that the cause of death was in doubt and could have been caused by external violence, or by cold from being in the water. If there was any question as to which of these had hastened Watkins's demise, the prisoner was entitled to a verdict of not guilty. However, if the jury acquitted him of the crime of manslaughter, the judge suggested that they could not acquit the prisoner of the assault. It was an assault for one man to strike another.

The jury found William Crocker not guilty of the manslaughter of George Watkins, but guilty of an assault, and the judge told him that the verdict was a proper one. Although the learned counsel for the defence had lightly described the occurrence at the beer house as no more than a drunken squabble, he did not consider this a very favourable description of this violent act. Regrettably, this was only one case resulting from quarrels 'occasioned by the love which the common people of this country have for intoxicating liquor.' A less compassionate jury would have found Crocker guilty of manslaughter and recommended him to be transported to Australia for life. Instead he was sentenced to six months' penal servitude.

10
'WHAT MARTHA'S ALREADY SAID GOES FOR NOTHING'

Crewkerne, 1843

Bachelor farmer Richard Alvin lived at Sheep Market Street, Crewkerne. In 1843, by the age of 30, he was said to be worth £18,000, an eccentric and something of a recluse, living with a spinster cousin Charlotte Coles and a servant, Martha Clarke, aged 20.

The household's apparently peaceful existence was soon to be hit by scandal. In May 1843, Martha accused 25-year-old Sarah Bulgin, an unmarried mother of two and Alvin's servant until about two years previously, of spreading false gossip about her, saying she had secretly borne an illegitimate child. Martha denied having done so and told Sarah to keep quiet, but not before rumours had reached the parish authorities. On 18 May, Martha was charged by John Turner, a local policeman, with having disposed of her infant. Protesting her innocence, she was lodged in custody at Turner's house.

One morning after breakfast, she broke down in tears. When Elizabeth, Turner's wife, tried to comfort her, she said that if she was had-up before the magistrates, she would confess everything. Mrs Turner asked her what she meant, and Martha admitted to having borne a child. If she was to suffer for it, then Alvin would as well. He had made her pregnant the previous year, and on the afternoon of Sunday 18 December, she gave birth to a baby in the hay loft of the house in Sheep Market Street. She knew that the child, whose sex she did not know, had been born alive as she heard it cry. Alvin, she said bitterly, delivered it and took it away, then sent her back into his house with orders to say nothing and carry on as if nothing had happened. His bitch had produced a litter at the same time and he prepared gruel for the animals, paying more attention to his dog than the mother of his child.

On his return home, the story was repeated to Mr Turner. Martha was taken before the town magistrates and a warrant was issued for Alvin's house to be searched for the child, or any traces of it. Turner checked the garden, hay loft and stables, but found nothing. Nevertheless, Martha's statement was enough for her and Alvin to be taken into custody at Taunton for questioning. As Turner took his prisoners to gaol, Alvin said nonchalantly, 'Never mind, what Martha's said already goes for nothing.' About a mile on, he said, 'I know all about it.' 'I should like to know all about it too,' Turner replied.

On being questioned at the gaol Alvin protested his innocence in relation to the birth or disposal of an infant, but Martha swore she had told the truth. However, unless a body could soon be found, there would be no case to answer.

On 10 June, after a visit by Mr Loveridge, one of the divisional magistrates, Martha made a statement indicating where she thought the child might have been buried. The next day, Hugh Simmonds, the local constable, John Turner and another police officer, William Pottinger, started digging in Alvin's garden. Buried below the bushes, about a foot below the surface, they found some bones, a skull, 'and remains like dung'. It was almost certainly the decomposed body of a small child. As Simmonds and the surgeon, Emmanuel Bowdage, took the corpse carefully out of the hole, they saw a band of straw was wrapped around it. They took it to the Red Lion Inn and placed in a storeroom to await the coroner's arrival.

At an inquest on 12 June, the jury decided 'that the body now found is the body of a human being, an infant, but how or by whom placed there is not known.' The magistrates opened their inquiry four days later in the Crewkerne Justice Room, and Richard Alvin and Martha Clarke were brought from the gaol through streets packed with people eager to catch a glimpse of them. Counsel for the prosecution was Mr Langworthy of Ilminster, while Alvin was represented by Mr Lowman and Mr Sparks. Nobody represented Martha Clarke.

Hugh Simmonds and William Pottinger testified to having found the body, and Emmanuel Bowdage recalled that on the previous Sunday afternoon, he had been called to Alvin's garden to see the body of an infant. It was taken to the Red Lion Inn and the next morning he had examined it in the company of a fellow surgeon, Mr Wills. The body was of a 'full grown infant much decomposed', he said, and twisted around it was a band of hay and straw. There were traces of blood on the band which he believed came from the child, and he said it must have been born alive; if it was stillborn there would have been no blood. It was too decomposed for him to say whether it had been a boy or a girl.

Sarah Bulgin said that during the previous year, she had noticed Martha getting larger. For a while they had worked as servants together until Sarah left, and one day, as they were gleaning corn together at the harvest, she had joked about Martha's appearance, but there was no response. One day a little later, Sarah had visited Alvin's house to find Martha Clarke looking smaller and ill. She made a remark to her about having 'lost her belly', but again there was no answer.

The next two witnesses, Mary Fowler and Charlotte Coles, were asked to confirm Martha Clarke's statement about some events on the afternoon of Sunday 18 December. Mary Fowler said she had been a servant to Mr Alvin's late father and had since married a local farmer. She knew Martha Clarke, but on the few occasions she had seen her recently, had observed no signs of pregnancy. However, on the morning of the Sunday in question, Miss Coles had called on her and said she was concerned about a rumour that Martha was expecting. Although Martha had immediately denied it, Miss Coles was unconvinced, and asked Mary Fowler to come to the house later that afternoon and have a look at the girl.

Mary said that at about 4 p.m. she called at the house, and while talking to Miss Coles in the hall, Alvin had walked past them. As a rule, he said hello to

Market Street, Crewkerne.

her and invited her to see the cows and the garden, but this time he did not seem pleased to see her there. Soon afterwards he went back out again. Mary then said that Miss Coles told her Martha was out milking the cows, and both women chatted for a while. About an hour later, she heard Martha come into the kitchen and begin pouring milk into a pail. Miss Coles then went out into the passage, and soon afterwards, Mary Fowler heard someone go upstairs.

When Miss Coles returned, she said Martha was not well and had gone to her room. A few moments later, someone called at the back door asking for Martha but when Miss Coles called up and told her, Mary Fowler heard the girl reply that if anyone wanted to see her they would have to come upstairs. It was then, Mary Fowler said, that Miss Coles asked her to go up and see what was wrong. The farmer's wife found Martha lying in bed complaining she had been feeling poorly since last night, after being out the day before with the donkey cart, running about and getting very warm. Afterwards she had stood about and got cold.

Suddenly Martha exclaimed, 'You know it had been reported a good deal about me that I be in the family way. Well I'm not! Here! feel me belly to prove it'. Taking her hand, the girl passed it over her stomach. Miss Coles had now arrived on the landing outside the room and called out to Martha that if she did not go downstairs at once, she would call the doctor to see her. The farmer's wife suggested to Miss Coles that they talk about the servant's condition before doing anything, and both women went down to the parlour to find Alvin sitting at the table.

When they discussed Martha's condition and the rumours of her pregnancy, Mary did not think Martha was with child. They wondered if she might have been confined elsewhere in the town but thought it unlikely, as her duties required her to be about the house and garden all day. Later, Mary continued, she took a cup of cocoa up to Martha and was followed by Miss Coles, carrying a candle.

While the girl drank, Miss Coles had stood holding the candle at the half-opened door, but when Mary came back onto the landing with the empty cup, Miss Coles asked if anything was wrong. Mary said she could not be certain, so Miss Coles had told her to go back and check the bed. Mary Fowler did so, and examined Martha's day clothes, finding some marks of blood, but put this down to natural causes rather than a concealed confinement. On returning downstairs, she told Miss Coles that she was sure the servant was not in the family way and went home at about 6.30 p.m.

Charlotte Coles stated that she lived with her cousin and managed his household. Martha Clarke had been in service for about two years, and until the rumours began before Christmas last, she had given no cause for complaint. Her duties included watering, feeding, milking and bedding down the household cows, sometimes with Alvin's help. Early in December, it had been rumoured that Martha Clarke was with child, but when asked whether it was true the girl had strongly denied it. However, Miss Coles explained, she was not completely satisfied because she thought Martha was looking rather stout, but when she had told the girl to do up her coat, she was able to do so. She therefore decided to ask Mary Fowler, as a former family servant and a respectable married woman with children, to look at Martha and give her opinion.

Miss Coles recalled that on the Sunday in question, Martha Clarke had had her lunch at 1 p.m., and then went into the back premises. She did not see her again until the milk was brought in later in the afternoon and she helped the girl to strain it into pails. Then, she said, Martha had complained of feeling unwell, and as the milk was taken down into the cellar she heard the girl go upstairs. She then recounted the events described by Mary Fowler. With regard to her cousin's activities during the afternoon, Miss Coles remembered that he was in and about the house and garden and did not leave the premises. She could not recall whether he had

The Square, Crewkerne, c. 1900.

helped with the cows or whether his behaviour to Mary Fowler was any different. Finally Edith Turner, the town policeman's wife, told of Martha Clarke's confession at her house but denied that she had induced the girl to make the statement.

After all the witnesses had been called, Richard Alvin was asked whether he wished to address the court. He said firmly that he was 'innocent of the charge.' Martha Clarke, sitting opposite, leapt to her feet and pointed at him, shouting, 'He is not innocent, gentlemen!' There was uproar in court for several minutes. When order had been restored, the chairman told Martha that if she wished to address the court, now was the time, but anything she said would be taken down and might be used against her 'in another place.' She told how she had given birth to a child, delivered by Alvin who then took it from her:

> He never allowed me to see the child and he would never tell me whether it was a boy or a girl because if no one saw it I should never blush if accused by anyone. As soon as I was delivered he told me to go down. I heard the child cry before and after I went down. I was in the hayloft about 10 minutes after the child was born and about 10 minutes after I was confined I went down and fetched the milking pail and brought it up to milk the cows. Alvin carried the milk as far as the kitchen door and I took it up and carried it in and placed it on the table. I then went up stairs and went to bed. I asked Miss Coles for some more clothes which she denied me and she said I should have no more. Mary Fowler afterwards brought me some which Miss Coles gave her. I had been in bed about half an hour when Mary Fowler came up to me. She examined me and heaved up the bedclothes and did not think there was any more the matter with me than with any other woman. Miss Coles was standing outside my bedroom. I saw Alvin place the hayband round something and heard it cry. It was moonlight at the time and there are windows in the place. When he was twisting the hayband his back was towards me, and after it was tied he threw it amongst the reed. I heard the child cry after I came down from the loft. I left him there and he returned about 5 minutes afterwards. I never heard the child cry after Alvin came down. He never told me where the child was but I suspected it was somewhere in the garden. The day after I was confined I went into the garden and saw the ground had been removed at the top of the garden near the middle walk but I never examined the ground. I was in the stable at the time I was taken in labour, and Alvin told me to go up into the hay loft and he said it was the best place. I never asked him what had become of the child.

Mr Alvin, she maintained, was the child's father. He had spoken to her a good deal about it, and said he knew what was the matter with her, but never mentioned that he should deliver it himself. She had provided the clothes for it and planned to entrust it to her sister to keep until she could care for it herself, as Alvin never suggested getting any clothes. Finally, she said, she never left his service, and the gate of the garden door was secured so that nobody could enter from the street.

There was further uproar in court once she had finished, and after the noise died down, the magistrates committed both prisoners for trial at the next Assizes

– Richard Alvin as principal in the murder and Martha Clarke as accessory after the fact. An application for bail for Alvin was refused, and both were taken to the County Gaol.

Alvin appeared before Mr Justice Coleridge at the Somerset Lammas Assizes in Bridgwater on 16 August 1843, indicted for 'the wilful murder of a child, name and sex unknown, on 18 December, 1842 in the Parish of Crewkerne, by tying a band of hay round its neck and thereby strangling it.' He pleaded not guilty. The charge against Martha of being an accessory after the fact had been dropped, and she was to be the prosecution's principal witness. Mr Kinglake and Mr Rawlinson appeared for the Crown and Mr Cockburn and Mr Stone defended.

Mr Kinglake opened for the prosecution by describing events leading up to Sunday 18 December. He told the court that the prisoner had lived in Crewkerne for some years and was a man of considerable property. The charge against him was that the female servant, who lived with the prisoner and his cousin, Miss Coles, was bearing his child, and that in December a child was born alive and he had killed it. The servant, Martha Clarke, affirmed that she was in the family way, the prisoner was the father and that on the afternoon of the Sunday before Christmas in 1842, she was delivered of a child. She would state that the prisoner knew she was expecting, that he had often spoken to her on the subject, and would give details of his actions on the afternoon in question. The substance of the indictment, Kinglake emphasised, depended upon the credit which the jury would place on the statement of Martha Clarke. The defence would doubtlessly seek to discredit her evidence as she had been an accomplice and party to the crime but, after hearing what she had to say, he would submit that she was not an accomplice.

The constable of Crewkerne and William Pottenger then gave evidence of finding the corpse. Mr Bowdage, the surgeon, spoke about its removal from the garden and his subsequent examination. Cross-examined by Mr Cockburn, he stated that he had not put the bones together or measured the child because it was too badly decomposed. He thought it had been in the ground for about six months, and he could not confirm whether it had been born alive. However, the blood found on the hayband might have flowed from the umbilical cord if it had been born alive, and it could also have been fatal if the cord had not been tied. He thought it unlikely that a woman just delivered of a child could carry a pail of milk, or even get up the next morning. In reply to a question from the judge, the surgeon conceded that 'women of the lower orders go to work sooner after delivery than those in the better classes of life.'

As principal witness, Martha repeated the evidence she had given at the previous proceedings. For the defence, Mr Cockburn subjected her to a searching cross-examination, and though she became confused about events in the hayloft, she stuck to her story. The remaining witnesses, Sarah Bulgin, Mary Fowler and Charlotte Coles, also repeated their evidence as given before the magistrates. Elizabeth Turner told of Martha's first statement and denied inducing or in any way encouraging the girl to confess.

Mr Cockburn then told the jury that the prisoner stood accused on the testimony of one witness, and he could not call evidence to prove that he was not a party to the 'transaction' with which he had been charged. His learned friend had pointed to the case depending entirely on the word of the principal witness, and if the jury did not believe her, that was the end as there was nothing in the rest of the evidence to fix guilt upon him. It was said that Martha Clarke was not an accomplice. What then was she? She had confessed to giving birth to a child and, when charged with having made away with it, blamed it on her master, the prisoner at the bar.

Taking each statement made by Martha Clarke in turn, he pointed out to the jury that there was no evidence as to the mode of death, and argued on the improbability of the mother of her firstborn child acquiescing in the contemplated murder of her infant in the hay loft, without remonstrating against the deed. Could a master have had so much influence over his servant to suppress a mother's feelings for her child and become a party to its death? The prisoner had no motive to kill the child; he was not poor and the expense of maintaining it would have been of no consequence. It might be said that his character was at stake, but he had no ground for fear of moral censure as he was unmarried and there was no reason why he should place himself in such dire peril of his life.

Cockburn suggested to the jury that there were three things on which they must be satisfied: first, that the child had been born alive; second, that the prisoner had killed it and third, that it was killed in the manner described in the indictment.

On the first point there was no evidence, except that of the witness, that the child had been born alive, and the surgeon could not be sure she was telling the truth. As to the second point, there was no evidence to connect the prisoner with the murder. With regard to the third, the jury must be satisfied that the death was occasioned in the manner described in the indictment, namely, that the prisoner had killed the child by tying a hayband around its neck, strangled and suffocated it. The evidence from the surgeon and the men who had discovered the body was that the hayband was tied round the body, but there was nothing to show that it had caused strangulation.

The defending counsel went on to say that that several actions by the prisoner proved his innocence. He had never tried to prevent Mary Fowler from examining Martha Clarke, even though he knew his cousin would be asking her to do so. Neither had the prisoner, after the first examination of his house and garden by the town policeman, removed the corpse to a more secret place. Mr Cockburn concluded by suggesting to the jury that the case was surrounded by great doubt and suspicion, and there was a total absence of motive for the prisoner to commit the crime.

In summing up, Mr Justice Coleridge told the jury that unless it was satisfactorily proved beyond all reasonable doubt that the death of the child had been caused in the manner described in the indictment, the prisoner could not be found guilty. If the jury believed that proof had not been given, it would be unnecessary for him to go through the whole of the evidence. It only took them a few minutes to decide that there was proof that the death had been caused by strangulation, and found Richard Alvin not guilty. Speculation remained as to whether Martha Clarke could have given birth to another man's child, on her own, in the hay loft, and buried the body under cover of darkness without anyone knowing.

11

'IT'S NO USE, I'VE DONE IT'

Weston-super-Mare, 1844

Joel Fisher of Weston-super-Mare was a veteran of the battle of Waterloo, having faced the Grand Army of Napoleon in 1815 as a member of the 7th Hussars. In 1844, aged 52 and back in civilian life, he had been the landlord of the Devonshire Inn on High Street for nearly three years. Born the son of a farm labourer in the nearby village of Wick St Lawrence, as a young man he had worked for Joseph Hewlett, a local farmer, before entering service with Mr Bisdee, a local surgeon. In 1811 he joined the army and served with honour until 1834 when the colonel of the regiment retired and he left the forces to act as the colonel's servant. He lived with him for nine months, before marrying a fellow servant. The couple set up home in Weston-super-Mare, where Fisher was re-employed by Mr Bisdee. Three children were born, but then the family was beset by tragedy. Mrs Fisher died, followed shortly afterwards by one of the children.

Fisher left Mr Bisdee, and soon afterwards, married Mary Hyatt, a widow with an adult son and daughter. The marriage was fiery from the outset. Mary had a violent, explosive temper and her children were prone to interfering. Within less than a year they parted for a few weeks, until Mary managed to persuade her husband to take her back, promising to behave better in the future.

For the next year the couple lived at Nailsea and Congresbury, but were soon quarrelling again. The fights were fuelled by Mary's daughter, who was living with the couple and actively took her mother's part against Joel. He bought the Devonshire Inn in 1841, using the nest egg he had accumulated during his army years. The squabbling with his wife continued unabated and Mary frequently left her husband, only to persuade him to take her back yet again. In 1843 she packed her bags once more, this time leaving with £20 of Joel's money and some linen. Furious, Joel managed to track his errant wife to Bath, where he recovered his money. By now his patience was all but exhausted, and he took out an advertisement stating that he would no longer be responsible for her actions.

It took only three weeks for her to wheedle her way back to Joel with promises that, if he took her back, she would control her temper and never leave him again. Her promises lasted until the long-suffering Joel had agreed to take her back yet again, when arguments resumed almost instantly. Soon he was at breaking point. As he was illiterate, he depended on his wife to manage the pub accounts. The pressure of running a busy public house and looking after his two young sons

High Street, Weston-super-Mare, 1920s.

grew too much to bear and, on Tuesday 4 June 1844, after one quarrel too many, he finally snapped.

On the previous evening, Joel and Mary had fought bitterly over Peter Baker, a lodger at the pub, who, according to Fisher, had left on account of Mary's conduct towards him. The argument blazed on, with Mary Fisher seemingly doing her best to antagonise her husband, blowing out his candles and erasing the details of the day's takings from the pub from the slate on which they were written. Throughout the argument, Fisher continually threatened to 'do for' Mary, and she refused to sleep with him, choosing instead to retire to bed with Ann Evans, a family servant, in the bedroom that the girl shared with Joel's two young children. Even after Mary had gone to bed, Joel continued to storm about in a state of rage, uttering threats that he would murder her and that that night would be her last. At one stage Fisher pounded on the bedroom door, ranting and raving, and Evans had to persuade his wife not to jump out of the bedroom window. Finally, at about 1 a.m., the fighting ceased and the pub fell quiet.

The silence was an uneasy one. Joel stayed awake throughout the night brooding until, at 5 a.m. the next day, he burst into the serving girl's bedroom, wielding an iron bar with which he had forced the door open. With his children, then aged about 10 and 12 years, screaming in the background and the servant girl begging him to go away, he dealt his wife several blows to the head with the iron bar, smashing her skull. He then left the room, returning shortly afterwards with a large carving knife and, standing on his wife's chest, proceeded to slash her throat so viciously that her head was almost severed. He then turned calmly to Ann Evans and reassured her that he would not hurt her – he had committed no sin, he maintained, merely removed a sinner from the world.

Weston-super-Mare from the Encampment, c. 1900.

Regent Street, Weston-super-Mare, c. 1900.

Satisfied that Mary was now dead, he left the room again and went immediately into the bedroom of William Upsall, one of the pub's lodgers, telling him exactly what he had just done. Upsall had been rudely awakened by the shouts and screams, followed by Joel Fisher rushing into his room, a bloody carving knife in his hands. Upsall asked if he had killed his children, to which Fisher jubilantly replied, 'No, but I've killed her!' He then asked Upsall to fetch a policeman.

By now the servant girl had alerted the neighbourhood to the situation at the inn. Meanwhile, Upsall had roused Mr Bernard, a local doctor and, having informed him of what had taken place, continued to the police station. Bernard arrived at the pub shortly before Constable Robert Hill, finding the door locked and one of Fisher's sons standing forlornly outside. Bernard had knocked on the door and Fisher had opened it. Seeing the boy, he had taken him gently back into the pub saying, 'Come in my son; it was for you I did it.' He had then bolted the door again behind him again, saying that he would admit nobody until the police arrived.

In answer to Constable Hill's knocking, Fisher had opened the door and led the two men to the bedroom where his wife's blood-soaked body still lay on the bed. As Mr Bernard bent over the corpse, Fisher began to mutter; 'I've done it; I've done it; it's no use; I've done it; I knew I should do it and I know I should be hung for it.' He was promptly arrested and taken to the police station at Weston-super-Mare. Hill then returned to the pub to carry out further investigations.

Having examined the dead woman, Bernard confirmed that the blows to the head had not killed her outright, but that the wound to her throat was the cause of death. Fisher later confirmed that he had cut his wife's throat because she was still breathing after his onslaught with the iron bar and he thought it best to put her out of her misery.

Fisher appeared at the Summer Assizes in Wells on 12 August 1844, charged with the wilful murder of his wife. Ann Evans, William Upsall, Constable Hill and Mr Bernard all testified before the court for the prosecution, and then it was the turn of Mr Cockburn, counsel for the defence to speak. He could not and would not deny that his client had committed the terrible act of murder, he said in his address to the jury, but he believed that certain features of the case should preclude a verdict of guilty of wilful murder which was not proven, he maintained, suggesting that the jury should consider instead a verdict of manslaughter.

He reminded the jury that Mary Fisher had had a violent and aggravating temper and that this may have provoked Joel Fisher to commit the crime. He pointed out that Fisher's actions immediately following the murder could not be described as those of a sane man. He had not harmed Ann Evans, the woman who had just witnessed his acts – on the contrary, he had almost encouraged her to bear witness against him. Fisher had then specifically requested that his lodger fetch the police. When the surgeon had arrived, he had opened the door only for long enough to allow his son to enter the inn, telling the boy that he had done this for him, even though the act had nothing to do with the child. Cockburn told the jury that this behaviour was without reason or sanity and pointed to madness in the accused.

Cockburn then called two witnesses to testify that Fisher's past behaviour had not always been rational. Joseph Hewlett, a local farmer, told of paying ten pennies for five pints of ale in the pub. The landlord had only taken eight of the pennies and, when Hewlett pointed out his error, had flown into a tremendous rage and threatened him with a carving knife. Hewlett purported to have been in fear for his life, although he was sure that Fisher had not been in control of his senses at the time and had not realised what he was doing.

The second witness, James Bailey Smith, was an excise man who had carried out regular excise surveys at The Devonshire Inn over the past three years. A certain strangeness about the accused had prompted him to comment many a time, 'That Fisher's mad.'

Tennis courts and putting greens, Weston-super-Mare.

The Hill and Promenade, Weston-super-Mare, 1925.

It was left to the judge, Mr Justice Pattison, to sum up the facts of the case for the jury. He instructed them to consider whether Mary Fisher had died from her wounds and, if she had, had the prisoner inflicted them? With regard to the defence, he reminded them that in the eyes of the law, a man must be considered sane and to know the laws of the land unless the contrary was proven. If a man did not know that what he had done was wrong, then he could be considered insane. If, however, he was aware that he had committed an act that was against the law and wrong, then he must be assumed to be responsible for his actions.

Given that Fisher had been muttering about being hanged for his part in the death of his wife, even while her body was being examined by the attending doctor, it was hard for anyone to argue that he had not understood that what he had done was both against the law and wrong. Thus the jury retired for only a short period before returning a verdict of 'Guilty of Wilful Murder.'

Fisher was then asked if there were any reason why he should not be given the death penalty, to which he replied that nothing had been said that ought not to have been and he would rather hang than live with such a wicked woman. He was well aware of what he had done, and could only hope that the Lord would have mercy on him as a sinner.

Mr Justice Pattison donned the traditional black cap and passed the death sentence. He then told Fisher that he was sorry to hear his remarks which, he felt, showed a 'fearful state of mind'. If Mary Fisher had indeed been as wicked as her husband stated, then he had sent her out of this world without the chance to repent and make her peace with God. He believed the jury had given the right verdict, and he hoped that Fisher would use the time remaining to him to come to a better state of mind since there was no hope of any mercy being extended to him on this earth.

While waiting to be transported from Wells to Taunton Gaol, Fisher was allowed to see his sons. Their last meeting was a painful one, at which Joel passed on his treasured Waterloo medal to the oldest boy, wishing fervently as he did that he had been killed in the field of combat so that his sons would not have been born into such disgrace.

Fisher's accommodation at Taunton Gaol was relatively pleasant, considering his circumstances. His cell was light and airy and had a small yard in which he could exercise, and an officer in constant attendance. He spent his last days in prayer or in long discussions with the prison chaplain. Two days before his execution, he received two visitors, his brother and an old army comrade, with whom he had served for twenty years in the 7th Hussars.

On the night before his death, the prison chaplain gave Fisher a letter of forgiveness, written by Thomas Hyatt, the son of his deceased wife Mary, and it apparently brought him great comfort. On 4 September 1844, after eating a light breakfast, he spent his last hours in prayer in the company of the prison chaplain. Divine Service began at 10 a.m., during which Fisher received the Sacrament. Then, escorted by the chaplain, prison officials and several of his comrades from Waterloo, he walked calmly and steadily to the scaffold. A crowd of 3,000 people assembled outside the prison to watch as the rope was secured around his neck and a hood placed over his head. A hush descended as the Lord's Prayer was recited and then, as the bolts were drawn, Joel was heard to cry out, 'Oh God, pardon my sins and receive my soul.'

The local newspaper reported that the prison governor had received numerous requests from people who wanted the dead hand of Joel Fisher to be rubbed over parts of their bodies. According to folklore, this was a recognised cure for both rheumatism and 'King's Evil', another term for scrofula or tuberculosis of the lymph glands. The paper expressed surprise that such superstition still existed.

12

'ASK HER FIRST IF SHE BELIEVES IN GOD?'

Bath, 1851

On Saturday 7 June 1851, a rather refined lady entered the shop of chemist James Searle in Claverton Street, Bath and enquired about an advertisement he had placed offering rooms to let. She was shown a small apartment and immediately agreed to move in for a week, possibly longer if her husband approved. Within two hours, she had returned with her luggage and settled in.

The Searles approved of their new tenant. Although obviously in the latter stages of pregnancy, she was well-dressed and appeared very respectable. Her husband arrived on 9 June, just in time for the birth of his daughter, Elizabeth, who was born on the following morning. The tenants, Mr and Mrs Slater, agreed to rent the small apartment for the next month and hired a nurse to assist Mrs Slater with the day-to-day care of the baby. However, at the end of June, Mr Slater spoke to the Searles, telling them that he would be vacating the rooms shortly to take his wife to London. He asked Mr and Mrs Searle if they would be prepared to care for the baby in their absence and an arrangement was struck between the two couples whereby Mrs Mary Searle would be paid 10*s* a week for caring for Elizabeth, plus an additional sum for washing.

Mr and Mrs Slater left Bath on 4 July. The baby proved to be a very fussy eater, often refusing food prepared by Mrs Searle. She rejected arrowroot, gruel and milk that had not been first diluted with water, but when the Slaters returned two weeks later to visit their daughter, they expressed their satisfaction at how well she was looking. They came back on 1 August and on this occasion, spent several hours alone with the baby before leaving again.

That evening, Elizabeth became ill with violent sickness and diarrhoea. She was given a saline mixture by Mr Searle and the next morning seemed much better, gradually recovering over the next few days. When her mother next visited, she was informed that her daughter had been poorly. After spending time alone with the baby, Mrs Slater went away again and almost immediately, the child suffered a recurrence of the sickness and diarrhoea. The Searles began to feel concerned, although they found it difficult to believe that a woman who seemed as respectable as Mrs Slater would deliberately harm her child. To be on the safe side, they spoke to a local surgeon, Mr Evan Evans, who suggested taking the child to the country for some fresh air. Mrs Searle's sister, Elizabeth Grant, who was staying with the Searles at the time, took the baby to stay with a cousin in Hilperton, Wiltshire.

Mrs Slater was surprised to find her baby absent when she next visited, but having been informed that this was on medical advice, she accepted the situation without complaint. However, on her return to London, she wrote to the Searles, asking for the baby to be brought back to Bath by Saturday 13 September, when she intended to visit again.

When the baby returned to the Searles' home, she had again been suffering from diarrhoea on the previous day. A surgeon was called as a precaution, and on examining the infant, Mr Lawrence found her to be thin and suffering from 'white mouth', with two small ulcers in her mouth caused by teething. Lawrence prescribed a mixture of borax and honey for the white mouth and some powders for the diarrhoea, the cause of which he attributed to a change in the child's diet.

Mrs Slater visited on 13 September as arranged and again spent time alone with her child. Two days later, she returned with her husband and the couple had a discussion with Mr and Mrs Searle about Elizabeth's illness. Mr Slater felt that the baby looked to be in good health and, when it was suggested that the child continue to be seen by Mr Lawrence, he pooh-poohed the idea, saying he felt that Mr Searle was quite capable of treating her himself.

Mr Lawrence met Mrs Slater on 20 September, and explained that Elizabeth had been quite poorly but was now improving and on her way to a full recovery. Again, Mrs Slater spent time alone with her daughter and once more the child suffered another bout of sickness and diarrhoea.

Mr and Mrs Searle were becoming increasingly concerned. On one occasion during Mrs Slater's last visit, baby Elizabeth had been seen to pull a wry face, as if she had just tasted something rather unpleasant. Mrs Slater had explained this by saying that the baby had vomited a little and that she had wiped her face with a handkerchief. However, the Searles were still very reluctant to make any direct accusations to Mrs Slater that she may be poisoning her baby.

After much consideration, Mr Searle wrote a letter to Mrs Slater, addressing it care of her solicitor, Thomas Crosby. In the letter he explained how ill Elizabeth had been following her recent visit, reassuring her that the baby's condition was now improving following treatment from Mr Lawrence. If anyone else but his family were caring for the baby, he wrote, he would think that the child was being administered something improper. Three days later, Mr and Mrs Slater were back and once again, their visit was followed by another bout of sickness and diarrhoea for baby Elizabeth.

By this time, all doubt had vanished from Mr and Mrs Searle's minds. The baby seemed in pain, so Mr Lawrence was called to examine her. Mrs Searle gave him two teats that had been used on the child's feeding bottles over the past few weeks. The Searles then contacted the police with their suspicions.

The police decided to conduct a covert surveillance operation on the occasion of Mrs Slater's next visit. Having instructed Mrs Searle not to leave Elizabeth alone with her mother at any time, Inspector John Norris and Eliza Lyons, a female searcher, positioned themselves in the chemist's shop, from where they

Searle's chemist's shop was in Claverton Street, Bath. (© Nicola Sly)

could watch the meeting through the blinds of a window in the wall dividing the shop from the parlour. Unfortunately, Mrs Searle was called away and in the short time during which she was absent, Mrs Slater and the baby moved out of the sight of the watchers at the window. When Mrs Searle returned, she, Mrs Slater and the baby went upstairs, quickly followed by Inspector Norris and Eliza Lyons. In a bedroom, the inspector informed Mrs Slater that she was to be taken into custody on suspicion of having administered something noxious to her child.

Mrs Slater begged the policeman to wait until her husband arrived on the three o'clock train, but to no avail. She was immediately placed in a cab and taken to the police station. On her arrival, she was searched. Nothing untoward was found about her person, so her gloves and pockets were taken for a more detailed examination.

Meanwhile, back at the Searles' home, baby Elizabeth was once more stricken with violent illness and, despite the best efforts of Mr Lawrence, her condition steadily deteriorated. She died on 11 October. A post-mortem examination was carried out by Mr Lawrence in the presence of several other doctors and also by Professor William Herapath, a foremost chemist and toxicologist of the day, and the results revealed traces of arsenic.

Lawrence found the child to be underweight to the point of emaciation. She had severe nappy rash and an ulcerated groin. Her internal organs were inflamed, consistent with the child having consumed numerous small doses of arsenic over a period of time.

The organs were removed and given to Herapath for further analysis. Traces of arsenic were found in baby Elizabeth's liver, stomach and intestines and also in the ulcer, which Mr Lawrence had dissected from the baby's groin. Slight traces were also found in a small patch of skin removed from her buttocks. In addition, Herapath tested a soiled nappy and a baby's nightgown, which bore splashes of vomit. Both items were also found to contain traces of arsenic. The most telling evidence was found on testing the two bottle teats, given to Mr Lawrence by Mrs Searle. Each contained some small crystals, which, when dissolved, tested positive for arsenic, albeit in very small quantities. As a result of the post-mortem examination and the subsequent testing of baby Elizabeth's organs, it was determined that she had died as a result of the repeated administration of arsenic over a period of time.

Police investigations into what was now a case of murder soon turned up some scandalous news about Mr and Mrs Slater. Mrs Slater was actually Elizabeth Catherine Lewis, a member of a respectable Bristol family, and who had previously worked as a governess. Her 'husband' was Mr Thomas Crosby, a well-to-do solicitor, also from Bristol. Baby Elizabeth was not Lewis's first child; she had travelled widely in the past, spending some years working as a governess in Barbados, and had another illegitimate child, a toddler allegedly fathered by a wealthy gentleman from the West Indies.

The couple were brought before magistrates at Bath who decided there was a case to answer against them, committing them to trial at the next Somerset Assizes. The trial opened at Taunton on 5 April 1852, with both defendants pleading not guilty to the murder of their daughter. Elizabeth Lewis was particularly vocal in her protestations of innocence, calling on God to be her witness and cursing the Searles, expressing a wish that every tear shed by her poor mother might rise up against them.

Mrs Searle was the first witness to be called and, for almost three hours, faced some very searching questions about her care of the baby and about the arsenic for sale in her husband's shop. She denied knowing where the store of arsenic was kept and, while acknowledging that she frequently helped her husband in his business and often dispensed medicines, vehemently denied the possibility that the bottle teats could have been accidentally contaminated. She was also asked about occasions in the past when her husband had made mistakes with prescriptions, but denied any recollection of Mr Searle being advised by a colleague to dispose of some drugs that had been dangerously mixed up.

Mr Searle then testified that the arsenic in his shop was kept in a stone jar, clearly labelled 'Arsenic – Poison'. The lid was tied down and the wooden spoon, with which the arsenic was measured, was kept inside the jar. The container was kept separately from other medicines, hidden away in a location that only he knew. He had signed a declaration stating that he would only sell arsenic to medical men and neither of his apprentices would ever touch the poison unless under his direct supervision. Like his wife before him, he too denied the possibility of any accidental contamination of Elizabeth's food.

Elizabeth Grant was called to testify about her stay in Hilperton with the baby. Before she could be questioned, Elizabeth Lewis called from the dock 'Will you ask her first if she believes in God?' That established, Grant related to the court

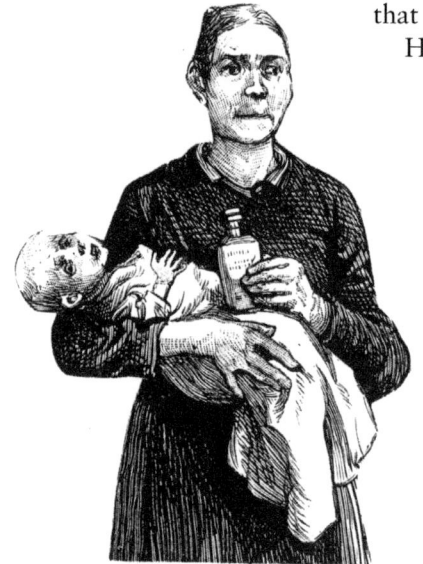

that the baby's health had improved considerably in Hilperton, although she had not seemed to gain weight.

Inspector Norris described the arrest of 'Mrs Slater' and the subsequent searches. He testified that no arsenic was found either on her person or in her gloves or pockets. Furthermore, none was found in any of the rooms at Claverton Street, nor at her home in Redland, Bristol, where she lived with her mother and sister. The police could find no evidence of arsenic being sold to either of the defendants. According to evidence later given by Mr Herapath, it was possible to test for one-millionth part of a grain of arsenic and, if there had been any traces of arsenic on Mrs Lewis's fingers, it would have been transferred to the gloves she had put on immediately after being apprehended in the bedroom at Claverton Street. If there had been arsenic on those gloves, then he would have found it.

Solicitors for the defence extolled the virtues of both Thomas Crosby and Elizabeth Lewis. It was pointed out that all the evidence against them was circumstantial and that neither had any motive for murdering their daughter. Baby Elizabeth was described as a placid child and Elizabeth Lewis was described as a kind, gentle and affectionate woman and a fond mother, who had often been distressed to the point of tears by her child's suffering.

Baby Elizabeth had suffered from sickness and diarrhoea while in the country with Elizabeth Grant, at a time when Lewis had not seen her. It was obvious to all that baby Elizabeth was a sickly child who frequently rejected food – she had an irritable stomach, the natural consequence of which was diarrhoea. The solicitors for the defence maintained that if the baby had been poisoned by arsenic, then the most likely source was contamination of her feeds deriving from the Searles' shop.

In summing up, Mr Justice Erle explained that while both prisoners stood charged with the wilful murder of their daughter, Thomas Crosby was only an accessory before the fact. He advised the jurors to think carefully about the evidence and not to deliver a guilty verdict unless they were convinced without reasonable doubt that the defendants were responsible for the death of their child. They should consider three questions; firstly, were they satisfied that arsenic poisoning had caused the baby's death? If they were not, then the only possible verdict would be not guilty, but if they were, had Elizabeth Lewis given the arsenic to the child? If she had, then was Thomas Crosby an accessory to the fact?

The jury took only a few minutes to consider the evidence and return a verdict of not guilty for both defendants. At this, Lewis slumped forward in a dead faint and had to be carried from the dock, followed by a tearful Thomas Crosby. Nobody else was ever charged in connection with the untimely death of baby Elizabeth.

13

'I DID IT FOR LOVE'

Frome, 1851

John and Leah Watts were dairy farmers living at West Woodlands, 2 miles from Frome. Their daughter Sarah, aged 14, helped with the chores at home, and when they went to town on market day to sell their wares, Sarah stayed behind to look after the house and farm. On Wednesday 24 September 1851, John and Leah set out for Frome as usual. Returning at about 4 p.m. they called out, 'We're home', as John Watts opened the front door, but there was no answer. He saw signs of blood on the kitchen floor, called again for his daughter, and then went through to the adjoining dairy. One of the dogs was lapping blood from the floor, where her dead body lay battered and bruised with her clothes torn. The remains of several broken basins suggested that she had put up a fierce struggle.

The devastated John picked her up and carried her upstairs. The police were notified, while the surgeon, Mr Giles arrived to examine the body laid out on the bed, and noted the extent of scratches on the neck and general bruising, as well as the fact that she had also been raped.

On 29 September, a detective, Mr Smith, appointed by the Home Office, was put in charge of the case. Several loaves of bread, plus some butter and cheese had disappeared, suggesting that Sarah had surprised a burglar. An upstairs room had been ransacked, while clothes and a watch were missing. On the kitchen table lay a silk handkerchief belonging to nobody in the family. When Smith examined the blood on the dairy floor, he also saw some spilt whey, and on checking the whey tub, he found signs of blood. On the dairy door was a handprint with blood on the thumb. A shoe mark on the wall matched a scuff mark on the victim's shoe.

No neighbours or passers-by had heard anything unusual, but the house was about a 100yds from the road. Sarah had last been seen, safe and sound, by neighbours at about 1 p.m. When others were questioned, it was revealed that three local men, Robert Hurd, William Sparrow and William Maggs, had all been drinking in a public house at around the time that John and Leah Watts were on their way to Frome. Sparrow knew the family well, and was probably aware of their market day routine, no least the time they were expected to return. He was therefore aware that Sarah would have been alone in the house at the time. At around midday, the three had been overheard making arrangements to meet in about an hour, and then went their separate ways.

Around 2 p.m. they were seen not far from, and in the direction of, the Watts' family home. Hurd was in front, encouraging the others on, but they were then seen without him. At about an hour later, a man was seen running away from the Watts' farm. Between then and the discovery of the body, they were noticed again but in different clothes, and Maggs was noticed passing something to Hurd. Later still they were all seen in the market place at Frome, and one of them was heard to mention 'a watch but no tin', which was taken as meaning that they had found a watch but no money somewhere. The other witnesses testified that a handkerchief left on the kitchen table belonged to Sparrow, though he denied having had a handkerchief for several years.

On 29 September, the day the detective started his investigation, there was a fair at North Bradley, 7 miles from Frome. Sparrow was there, and a Mrs Watson said to him that as he was from Frome, he must have heard about the murder. He told her that he knew about it, as he had seen the victim since she was killed. She had been lying near the whey tub with her dress over her head, and blows on her head had been inflicted by a stick, and she had been in the whey tub which had been covered with blood from her head, 'and that he did not think it would ever be found out, as only one man had done it, and he would never tell.' Amazed that he should know all these details, Mrs Watson asked if he knew how the murder had been committed. He then described to her how Sarah had been hit with a stick, held in the whey tub until dead, and then left on the floor. At the time, the detective had yet to discover all this for himself, and so naturally none of it was yet public knowledge. There was only one way that he would have known, and that was for him to have been there at the time – either as an accomplice, or as the killer himself.

At about the same time, Maggs was overheard telling somebody else that he knew Sparrow was going to 'peach' on his associates, so he could be pardoned and claim a £50 reward. Sparrow, Maggs said, would be unable to do so, as he had killed the girl when she recognised him. The detective also gathered that Hurd had been the mastermind of the bungled robbery, but after the initial planning, merely acted as an accomplice of the others.

On 30 September, Sparrow was arrested as he had a watch in his possession, assumed to be the one taken from the Watts' house. He claimed he had bought it from Hurd in the presence of Maggs, and this led to the arrest of all three. No owner for the watch was ever found, but it gave the police officer a good enough excuse to arrest them. Sparrow was further questioned by the detective, who noticed Sparrow's hand was bandaged. Asked how he had injured his hand, he said that it had been bitten in an argument he was involved in the previous day. When the wound was examined, it was apparent that it had been inflicted several days before.

Also on 30 September, the coroner, Mr Ashford, held an inquest at the George Inn, West Woodlands. Whether the cause of death was a blow to the head or strangulation was open to doubt, but after a further post-mortem, he deduced that pressure on the windpipe had killed her. When the coroner asked, rather oddly whether she could have strangled herself, Giles said that this was impossible, and the size of the bruises around her neck suggested the fingers of a man's hand. As yet, there was insufficient evidence to pin the murder on any individual, and the jury were instructed to return an open verdict that the deceased was wilfully murdered by person or persons unknown.

On 27 October, the three men were brought before the magistrates' office at Frome. Alongside them was a fourth, Sergeant, who had been seen with them and had been arrested by Smith that morning. Several witnesses were called, among them Sophia Cornish, whose husband William was an innkeeper at Frome, and Mary Francis, whose husband kept the Horse and Groom at West Woodlands. All of them could account for the movements of some, if not all four prisoners on the day of the murder, and the magistrates were left with the impression that each man had made a point of being seen, preferably with somebody else, in order to establish an alibi and thus be nowhere near the Watts' farm when Sarah was killed. No conclusive evidence was proven, but the prisoners were remanded in custody for a further period.

As the prosecution wished to call for forty-three witnesses, gathering the evidence proved a lengthy process and the case did not reach court for almost six months. On 6 April, Sparrow, Maggs and Hurd were brought before Mr Justice Erle at Taunton Assizes, with Mr Edwards leading the case for the defence, Mr Moody and Mr Everitt, the counsel for the prosecution. The main facts of the case rested upon circumstantial evidence; the combined evidence of the witnesses for the prosecution proved inadequate, and they all swore to having seen the prisoners elsewhere in Frome at the time the murder was committed. When Mr Edwards addressed the court at the end, he said that in his view, a weaker case had never been submitted before a jury. Was there evidence, he asked, upon which they would even hang a dog? In particular, the watch that had led to the prisoners' arrest was not the one stolen from the Watts' house, and there was nothing to suggest that it had not been obtained in a perfectly legitimate manner. It took the jury little time to hand down a verdict of not guilty against all three.

The case against Hurd and Maggs was demonstrably lacking, but in view of what almost amounted to a confession at North Bradley fair, Sparrow was perhaps fortunate to be acquitted. He had been seen near the scene of the crime, had an unexplained bite mark on his hand, and had left his handkerchief on the kitchen table.

Yet the sad tale was not yet over. During the initial investigation, suspicion had fallen briefly on another youth, Joseph Seer. Soon after the murder, he left the area, joined the army, and was invalided out about ten years later. On the morning of 17 September 1861, he reported to the police station at Frome to have a form filled in which would enable him to get his three months' pay on being discharged. The magistrates' clerk, Mr Turner, thought he seemed very ill-at-ease while filling in the form. Asking if anything was the matter, Seer said he had a confession to make.

'I murdered Sarah Watts,' he told Turner and Superintendent Deggan, in the latter's office. 'I hope the God above will let me live to see her again in another world. I have [had] it on my mind a long time. I have been very unhappy ever since.' He said he had known her and played with her as a child. He knew that her parents would be out of the house as it was market day, and he thought her father was 'worth some money'. Going to the house at about 3 p.m., he asked her where to find the money, but she would not tell him. He offered to marry her and take her to America, but she told him firmly that the money did not belong to him. 'If you don't tell me where it is I will be the death of you,' he insisted, taking hold of her by the neck and beating her on the head with a poker. He then dragged her body into the dairy, and put her in the milk pail, leaving her for dead. He then removed 2s from a cup on the mantelpiece, searched the rest of the house, and helped himself to some clothes before leaving. As he knew he was under suspicion of murder, he ran away to sea, and later enlisted in the army. 'I have now got it off my mind,' he concluded. 'I killed her for love. I was very fond of her.'

Within a week, further information emerged. As he had given his age at the time of his discharge from the army as twenty-five, he could only have been about fifteen at the time Sarah was killed. He had evidently laid low for a few years afterwards, as he did not enlist until December 1857. In June 1859, he embarked with his regiment for Corfu, where he became mentally unbalanced and twice attempted suicide. He was sent home and in August 1861, admitted to Fort Pitt, a military mental hospital at Chatham. One month later he was discharged as 'a hopeless lunatic and unfit for further service', sent back to Frome under escort, and handed over to the care of friends.

After his confession, he was taken into custody at Shepton Mallet Gaol, and brought before Frome Magistrates' Court on 8 October. The main witness, an elderly cooper, James Payne, testified to having known Seer since the latter was a child. A few days after the murder, Payne went into the Castle Inn to meet his wife. Seer came in, evidently drunk. Mrs Payne and a friend were talking about the incident and Seer, overhearing them, said he 'had done all he could with the woman [sic] and then he murdered her because he should never be found out.' Payne should have told someone else about it at the time, but when he left the inn to look for a constable to whom to report the matter, his wife (now deceased) ran after him to warn him that if he did so, 'you will be murdered as sure as you be born.'

Further, but less conclusive, evidence came from four other witnesses. One recalled having seen a man who came to her house shortly after the murder, but she could not be certain whether the prisoner was the same man. The other three could add nothing of importance, being either reluctant to say anything at all, or else only having vague recollections of having ever seen the prisoner shortly before or after the murder. What purpose they served in being called at all was debatable. The chief constable applied for a remand and Seer was kept in custody.

When proceedings were resumed on 12 October, Mr Bartrum, defending, said that the prisoner, 'a hopeless lunatic', was 'not responsible for his own acts.' The bench said that that he 'had occasioned very considerable trouble', and Mr Simkins, the gaol surgeon, testified that he could not find in Seer any trace of insanity. However, Superintendent Deggan then produced a letter from the India Office, London, stating that Seer was apprenticed to the East India Company to serve in the Indian Navy in 1847 for seven years. He had arrived at Bombay in December 1847, and was discharged in July 1854. He was therefore not in England when Sarah Watts was murdered, and could have known nothing about the crime. His confession could only be explained by his 'diseased state of mind'. The Earl of Cork, chairman of the magistrates, concluded the trial by discharging him, admonishing him on his folly and the wickedness of his conduct, which had made so much trouble for the police and bench, and so great an expense at the county, and told him firmly never to repeat such conduct.

14

'WE'LL FIND THE BODY YET'

Simonsbath, 1858

William Burgess of Simonsbath, Exmoor, was an agricultural labourer by profession. He was known in the neighbourhood as a man of difficult character. One employer who took him on to look after his animals on Exmoor told him one day that 'if he did not take care, he would come some day to end his life on the gallows.' He worked for several different farmers at various times, and was rarely without a job, but too ready to spend all he earned on drink.

Around 1840, he married a woman who was careful with their finances and good at saving. It appears that she was a good influence on him, and managed to keep him from the bottle at least part of the time. They made their home at Slate Quarry Cottage, and between them they raised three children, Tom, Emma and Maria (sometimes known as Anna Maria, Hannah, or even Hannah Maria. According to one contemporary account there were five children altogether). Once, after a heavy bout of drinking, he decided that they would emigrate to the United States of America. He sold most of his goods and left Exmoor on his own for Bristol, intending to look for a berth on board a ship. Once he reached America, he said, he would send for his wife and family. Instead, he went to Wales, on a drinking spree, and stayed in several public houses until his money had almost run out. Returning home, he used most of his remaining funds to buy back some of the goods he had recently sold, and hit the bottle again.

When the Revd William Thornton, the kindly new priest of the ecclesiastical parish of Exmoor, was appointed to the Church of St Luke and moved into the parsonage at Simonsbath, the opportunity was too good to miss. Thornton was only twenty-seven, full of youthful zeal and naturally keen to help. Burgess came to the parsonage one day, claiming to have suffered great misfortune after a pig and a pony had just died, neither of which he could afford to lose. Would the parson be so kind as to help him by drawing up a 'brief', or begging letter, so he could take it around with him and seek donations for buying a couple of animals to replace them? As Burgess was illiterate, the Revd Thornton eagerly prepared the letter and headed the subscription list by contributing a guinea.

Soon afterwards, the well-meaning Thornton learnt that the pig and pony had died five years earlier. He was prepared to put it down to experience, until an influential parishioner accused him of aiding and abetting a notorious rogue and suspected sheep-stealer in his efforts to obtain money by false pretences. It was an unpromising way for a clergyman to start with a new parish. Needless to say, Burgess exploited the letter to the full, taking it around the parish and even further afield. Having collected a generous amount from the sympathetic and the gullible, he spent it all in the taverns of South Molton.

On returning to Simonsbath, he soon learned that his little ruse was the talk of the area, and Thornton was furious at having been duped. The latter often went riding in the countryside, and it was difficult for both men to avoid each other. Nevertheless, Burgess prudently did his best, and every time he saw the vicar coming his way, he would turn aside or leap over a fence in order to avoid meeting him.

By this time Mrs Burgess, who had never been strong, was at the end of her tether. Having tried to reform her husband but failed, she became thoroughly depressed and unwell, caught measles, and gave up the fight for life in January 1858. Because of his bad reputation, it was whispered that she had met her end at the hands of her violent husband. It was fortunate that Mr Spicer, 'a highly respectable medical gentleman' (if not a doctor) from North Molton, and a nurse, Rebecca Barwell, had tended her during her last days and vouched for the fact that she had died of natural causes.

Thornton was full of Christian forgiveness. On hearing the news, he went to Slate Quarry Cottage and asked if there was anything he could do. Burgess told him sadly that the home would have to be 'broken up', and he would need to try and place the children into service locally. His bad reputation had gone before him, and he had to make several abortive attempts, the children being refused by several people who regarded the Burgess family as bad news. One family involved was struck by tragedy shortly afterwards. Burgess visited James and Sarah Hayes at their house, South Hill, near Withypool, and asked them if they would accept Anna. They declined, as they already had one small child and Sarah was expecting another. When the house caught fire soon afterwards, James and Sarah escaped unhurt, but James's elderly father John, and two others staying there at the time, Matthew and Grace Shapland, died from suffocation and burns.

At last Tom and Emma were accepted by a family at South Molton. Little Anna, aged 5 or 6, was too young, and had to stay with her father when he found lodgings for himself on the outskirts of Simonsbath with the Marley family. They lived at Gallon House Cot, so named as it adjoined the Gallon House Inn, where beer was sold by the gallon. Each week he had to pay 2s 6d for Anna's maintenance – money which he begrudged spending on her, rather than in the inns.

On the evening of 24 July, he asked Mrs Marley to prepare the few clothes Anna had, as he was intending to take her to stay with his sister at Porlock. In the small hours of Sunday morning he awoke, dressed quickly, roused the girl, and they left the house. He visited his sister, taking with him the bundle of children's clothes – but was on his own. That afternoon he returned to Gallon House Cot, still alone, and stayed there until the following Thursday, when he said he was also going to move to Porlock. He had not been seen since. Shortly after his disappearance, Mrs Marley had inspected the ashes of a fire at the back of the lodgings, and noticed the remains of clothes. She identified a piece of scorched calico as coming from Anna's spare frock, and immediately suspected the worst.

Soon afterwards Thornton, riding into Simonsbath, found Mr Vellacott, the parish clerk, and Mr Court, the forester, having an animated discussion about the mysterious disappearance of young Anna Burgess. She was nowhere to be found, and everyone suspected her father had 'done her in'. Thornton feared that they were right, but he warned them that it was unwise to make such an allegation unless fully supported by evidence. Nevertheless, they both told him that the girl had not been seen for ten days.

After a troubled night, Thornton sent for Court, and asked him to go on his (Thornton's) horse to Porlock, look in on old Mrs Burgess, make it appear as casual as possible, and to keep an eye out for Anna but not to say anything about her. Court did so, and returned that evening to say there was no sign of the girl anywhere. Thornton's suspicions hardened and he went to visit Mr Fry, the parish constable, and asked him to go to Lynmouth, where he thought it likely that an unsuspecting fisherman might have ferried Burgess over to Wales. Next he went back to Forest and asked him to get hold of all the men that he could and organise a thorough search for Anna Burgess, though they would more likely be looking for a grave than a missing child.

Unable to sleep that night, Thornton got up before dawn to ride the forty miles to Curry Rivel, near Taunton, the home of Superintendent Jeffs, the chief police officer of Somerset. After a brief meeting, both men rode back to Simonsbath, where they arrived just before noon and were greeted by a group of people near Gallon House. They said they had found the grave, but it was empty. Thornton and Jeffs asked the men to lead them to the spot, where they saw 'deads', or ridges of yellow earth thrown up by mineral prospectors. There were obvious signs of disturbance, and as they moved the earth, they found a small neatly cut grave with the sods carefully laid on top. Though they had dug into it, there was no body to be found.

There was to be some compensation for this disappointment. On returning to Simonsbath, Thornton and Jeffs were greeted with the news that Fry's enquiries at Lymouth had revealed that Burgess had indeed found a fishing boat to take him across to Swansea. Jeffs and Fry went down to Lynmouth in a pony trap, announcing their intention of taking a boat themselves to go after their suspect. The parson's intuition had been right, and he was more than ever convinced that little Anna's body would be found somewhere beneath the soil. Even so, he asked the men to continue searching and enquiring around the district in case there had been any sightings of her, dead or alive.

Another unsuccessful day of looking followed, and an exhausted Thornton retired to bed early. He was awakened at midnight by the sound of stones against his bedroom window. Opening the window and looking out, he met the gaze of several of the search party, who told him that they had got Burgess. Jeffs and Fry stood by the door as Thornton quickly dragged some clothes on and went downstairs. He told the prisoner quietly that as his clergyman he would do all he could, 'but you must tell me what you've done with Anna.'

Burgess stubbornly said nothing. The patience of an exhausted Thornton finally gave way as he called him a murderer, and angrily told the crowd standing around that 'his silence convicts him.' It was now Jeffs' turn to be angry, as he told the parson that he had damaged their case severely by letting Burgess know that they still had not found Anna. 'We'll find the body yet,' Thornton assured him, a little hesitantly.

When the policemen had searched Burgess, they found a pair of child's boots in his pocket which Mrs Marley identified as belonging to Anna. This, they felt, was sufficient reason for taking him into custody under the magistrates at Dulverton while they continued to make enquiries. Meanwhile, the search for Anna's body continued. At length, the magistrates warned that they could not hold the prisoner indefinitely, and a body must be produced soon or they would have to release him for lack of evidence. Burgess knew that as long as he kept silent while being questioned, and did not tell anybody where the body was, he would soon be free.

Just in time, a man came forward with what he assured them was vital evidence. The price of his information was a guarantee that his identity would never be revealed. He came to see Thornton and told him about the 'deads' on a trackway to the Wheal Eliza mine. The man and one of his friends were familiar with the trackway, and had noticed what might be a grave among the 'deads' there. A slaughtered sheep had probably been buried in the spot, as sheep stealers were in the habit of burying a carcase in such places, return for it under cover of darkness, and then cut it up in a nearby cottage for clandestine distribution. Both men intended to dig there that night; they may have been sheep stealers themselves, hence the request for anonymity. He confided that they had told a third man that they thought they had found a sheep buried, and invited him to share the spoils.

Thornton asked the name of this third man. Far from keeping his identity a secret, the informant was prepared to tell him that it was none other than William Burgess. The latter was still in captivity and therefore unable to get to the scene, but police time was running out and there was a good chance that within a few days he would be freed. There was one more important part of the story to come. One night in June, the man and his companion had arranged to meet Burgess and dig the carcase up between them. Burgess and the other man had not turned up, and the informant was there on his own, when he heard footsteps. Somebody was going in the direction of Wheal Eliza mine, which had not been worked for some years. All this happened in the last week of July, when Anna Burgess went missing.

Thornton's intuition had served him well once already. He promptly rode to Dulverton, told the magistrates everything he had learned, and that he was convinced they would find the body in the mine. They promised they would have the mine pumped and searched. Even if nothing was found, they were prepared to meet any costs involved. In the meantime, Burgess would remain in custody.

The shaft was filled with water to a depth of about 220ft, but the magistrates kept their word. Work was begun on 16 October, the shaft was pumped and almost empty, when a mechanical fault in the machinery resulted in the mine being filled again. By 2 December, the job was completed, and it was possible to descend the shaft. Not surprisingly, the call was 'send for Parson Thornton'. He arrived, and asked for a volunteer among the crowd who had come to watch out of curiosity. A young man stepped forward, and a strong rope was tied around him as he carefully descended the old and rotten ladder. In case it gave way, twenty men were holding onto the rope. Fortunately there were no accidents, and at last they were satisfied that the man had reached the mine floor. Presently they felt a tug on the rope, and in due course, the face of the man appeared. In his arms he was holding a large parcel tied with cord. Once he had climbed out and the rope was untied, Thornton took a knife and cut the cord. An old coat, presumably

St Luke's Church, Simonsbath.

belonging to Burgess, fell away, revealing a bag outside another bag. At length he found the remains of a child's body, covered by a shift. The face had gone.

The body was carried into a nearby cottage. Thornton put the pitiful remains inside, locked the room, and then sent a man on horseback to Dulverton with the news they had long dreaded. A little later three doctors, policemen, a magistrate and coroner arrived. With them came Mrs Marley, who was able to identify the child's corpse by the hair and shift as Anna Burgess. The coroner asked Thornton to stay with the doctors while they conducted a post-mortem. Her body was so badly decomposed that it was impossible to prove conclusively how she had died, and concluded that she must have been either strangled or battered to death. After the macabre proceedings, Thornton was entrusted with her remains for a Christian burial, and later that day she found rest at last in the churchyard at St Luke's.

On 4 December, five miles away in Exford, the Monckton coroner, William Webber, held an inquest on Anna. The verdict, a foregone conclusion, was wilful murder by William Burgess, and he was taken from Dulverton to Taunton Gaol. Overcome with remorse, he tried to cut his throat with a pair of scissors, and was then watched by the prison staff to prevent him from a second attempt. A few days later he stood trial at Somerset Assizes, and was charged with murdering his daughter on or about Sunday 25 July. Thornton was among those called to give evidence. Burgess was found guilty by Mr Justice Byles, and sentenced to death.

Burgess agreed to receive Thornton in the prison cell, but would not look at him. During their meeting he stood with his face to the wall, his arms over his head. He made a full confession, which appeared later in the *Taunton Courier*; 'I murdered my child for the purpose of saving 2s 6d per week, that I might be enabled thereby to indulge myself in more drink; and to indulge in drunkenness

I committed the awful deed. Do you, Sir, go back to Simonsbath, and tell the drunkards there to forsake drunkenness and strong drinks, or they may yet stand a condemned felon, as I now stand.' Burgess was illiterate and this was no written confession, but presumably it was a reporter's transcription of Thornton's words. Quite often, he said, he could not find the money, and Mrs Marley continually 'pestered' him for it. Anna was in his and everyone else's way, and he thought she 'would be better out of it.' The horrified Thornton was lost for words. At length Burgess looked round for the first time, and said he wanted to see his other children. He loved Emma, he admitted brokenly, almost as much as her little sister.

Without another word, Thornton turned round to leave the cell, but Burgess insisted on shaking his hand, saying that though the parson had hunted him, he was a real friend. Thornton then rode to Simonsbath, had a meal, saddled another horse, and rode to North Molton where Tom and Emma were in service. They knew nothing of what had happened since they last saw their father, and to the parson fell the painful duty of telling them that their father was going to be hanged for the murder of their little sister.

He started by seeing Tom alone and telling him that his sister Anna was dead. Tom looked at him and asked if father had killed her. Thornton nodded, and the boy said he always thought he would. Neither he nor Emma wanted to see their father, but Thornton persuaded them to change their minds, and personally made the travelling arrangements. When the prison governor brought them into the cell, Burgess broke down and wept.

He had one more statement to make while under sentence of death at Taunton. The fire at South Hill in January which had resulted in the death of John Hayes and two other people in the house was no accident. According to a descendant of the Hayes family, Burgess admitted that he had set fire to the dwelling in revenge for their refusal to take Anna in.

On the night of Thursday 6 January 1859, the last of his life, Burgess was very restless. After a troubled sleep, he saw the prison governor at 6 a.m. the next day and the chaplain visited him a little later. At least twice that morning the prisoner was seen in his cell on his knees, deep in prayer. After breakfast he was led to the prison chapel for a short service with the other prisoners. Afterwards he was received by the hangman, William Calcraft, at the chapel door, and executed shortly after 9 a.m.

15

'NOTHING HAS EVER BEEN ADMINISTERED TO HER IN HER FOOD'

Yeovil, 1860

Silvester Peters was a linen draper in Yeovil, where he and his wife Sarah lived over the shop. Aged 31 in 1860, he and Sarah had a 2-year-old daughter, Augusta Matilda. Sarah had never been strong, and her health had deteriorated further since the birth of their child. Throughout the spring and summer of 1860, she was left progressively weaker after severe attacks of violent vomiting and diarrhoea. Their physician, Dr Garland, thought she had an 'intense irritation of the stomach and bowels of an obscure nature'. She did not respond to treatment, and by the end of June, he was so alarmed by her condition that he sent a sample of her urine to be analysed by Professor William Herapath, and the results revealed traces of antimony. Suspecting deliberate poisoning, on 2 July, he passed the report to Mr Smith, the Yeovil police superintendent.

When Dr Garland visited her the next day and checked whether she was still taking the medicine, he was surprised to be told by Peters that she had ceased to do so on his instructions. He hoped the doctor would not be offended, but he thought it better that she should stop. Garland told him that he could see no improvement in her condition, and in view of Herapath's report, said he should come and see her again the next day. Mr Peters asked him not to, as doctors' visits were very expensive, but changed his mind when Garland said he was prepared to visit as a friend without charging an additional fee.

On the evening of 4 July, he returned to their home and found Sarah in extreme agony. Throughout the night he applied every remedy he could think of that would help, but it was to no avail. Shortly after 1 a.m. she was dead.

An inquest was opened at the Mermaid Inn on July under the coroner D.H. Ashford. First to be called as a witness was Dr Garland, who told the jury that he suspected her death was not from natural causes, and presented Herapath's letter referring to the tests on the sample. Ashford then adjourned the inquest, and despite protests from Mr Peters's solicitor Mr Glyde who thought it unnecessary, he ordered a post-mortem on the deceased. The man originally chosen for the task, Mr Jay, a surgeon from Queen Camel, was away at the time, and the post-mortem was carried out by Mr Winter Walter, a surgeon from

Stoke-sub-Hamdon, assisted by Dr Garland and his partner, Dr Thorpe. Also present was Dr Russell Aldridge, West Coker surgeon Mr John Moore, and representing Silvester Peters's interests, Dr Taylor Warry.

On the resumption in the Mermaid on 24 July, Mr Walter gave evidence that Mrs Peters's lungs revealed that she had had consumption. There were many tubercles (nodules on the bones, skin or lungs indicating tuberculosis) present, and signs of extensive mesenteric disease in the abdomen. In her liver, the duodenum and the colon were held together by massive inflammation which indicated an abscess had breached the colon, allowing some of its contents to escape into the peritoneum. The resulting peritonitis had caused her death, though in view of her poor state of health, she would not have survived for more than a few weeks. Mr Walter stated that he could find no trace of poison in the body, but at the request of Dr Garland, the stomach and internal organs were sealed in jars and passed to Superintendent Smith, who took them to Herapath.

When Dr Garland was recalled to the witness box, he confirmed Walter's findings, and agreed that the condition of Sarah Peters's body was very emaciated. Nevertheless, he thought the perforation of the colon might have been caused by the administration of some noxious substance.

Next to give evidence was Herapath, who confirmed that the sample of urine taken from Sarah Peters contained antimony, but stated there was no sign of the poison or any other metallic or mineral irritant in the organs sent to him. The stomach was inflamed in two places in a patchy manner, as were two places in the intestines, which generally indicated cases of irritant poisoning. In instances of a general inflammatory disease, he said, the whole organ would be inflamed. Inflammation produced by an irritant was influenced by the nature of the substance, and if solid, it would operate in a very local place but if fluid, it would only act in the lower portions of the organ. In his opinion, there was sufficient inflammation in the stomach and intestines to have caused death.

When asked why, if antimony was found in the dead woman's urine, there was no sign of the poison in her tissues, he said that in the few days which had elapsed between the sample and death, there had been enough time for the poison to pass out of the system. He assumed that the antimony had passed away, even though the appearance of the intestines indicated an irritant had been at work.

Nevertheless, when questioned by one of the jurors, he admitted that out of the many livers he had examined over the last twenty years of his professional career, he had never seen one in such a poor condition as that of Mrs Peters, and this must have been the result of a long standing disease; moreover, he had never known antimony to be a cause of death. He qualified this last remark by pointing out that it had not yet been discovered how long antimony remained in the body, or how long it took to disappear, as it had only recently been identified as a poison. He also pointed out that antimony was sometimes given medically to induce vomiting, but the inflammation seen in Mrs Peters's organs would never have been produced by such small doses.

On being recalled again, Dr Garland confirmed that he had not prescribed any medicine which contained antimony. Sarah Peters had told him that the sickness came on almost immediately after she had taken gruel, or the arrowroot he had prescribed, and complained that the medicine was making her ill. He said that

High Street, Yeovil, c. 1910.

he had assured her this was impossible, as the preparation he was giving her was one of the strongest against sickness. Dr Garland asked Sarah how soon she was sick after taking her medicine and she replied that it was within half an hour, but then told him that she took some gruel during this time. The doctor gave her some more medicine, waited with her for half an hour and then told her not to take anything for another hour. When he called the next morning, he found Mrs Peters had had no sickness.

Dr Garland said that after her death, he had suggested to the widower that an examination should be held. Silvester Peters had taken violent exception to this, declaring that he would rather have his own bowels opened than his wife's body touched. Despite Garland's assurances that he had no suspicion of anything untoward, Peters still refused to give his consent. During their conversation, the latter suddenly said, 'You know Mr Garland, nothing has ever been administered to her in her food.' Rather surprised, the doctor left the room, but returned after consulting his partner to say he had received the report from Mr Herapath indicating poison in the urine sample, and he could not issue a death certificate as he did not know how poison came to be in the system. Yet Mr Peters still refused to permit an examination, and said he would obtain a certificate from Dr Tomkyns, another physician in the town. At this stage Dr Garland went to the police.

During the proceedings, Mr Langworthy, a solicitor from Ilminster acting for Mr Peters, had asked questions of the witnesses from time to time seeking clarification of the evidence. He now asked for the recall of Mr Walter, and wished to know how many perforations he had seen in the intestines. The surgeon replied that he had found two or three which he concluded had been caused by the escape of matter from the large abscess and did not arise from anything within the organ.

The inquest was adjourned once again to the following Saturday 28 July, to allow the other medical men who had attended the post-mortem to give evidence. As coroner and jury re-assembled in the Mermaid Inn at 10 a.m., evidence was taken from Dr Aldridge, who confirmed the findings of his medical colleagues and said he thought that the inflammation and resulting peritonitis was caused by disease, but the administration of an acute irritant could cause peritonitis. In reply to a question from

Mr Langworthy, he answered that Mrs Peters had suffered from a consumptive disease 'of long standing', and had been ill for three years. The symptoms of sickness were usual in such an illness. The cause of death, he considered, was 'disease of the liver and mesentric glands, and from the subsequent formation and giving way of an abscess'.

Doctors Warry and Thorpe and Mr Moore, the surgeon, next said they believed death was the result of peritonitis. To support his opinion that the vomiting from which Mrs Peters suffered was the result of her general illness, Dr Warry stated that her husband had given him a letter she had written on 24 May, while she was staying at Worle, near Weston-super-Mare, telling him she was having bouts of sickness. However, Mr Moore was not sure of the cause and could not account for the patchy nature of the inflammation, suggesting it could be the result of an irritant such as antimony.

When the jury adjourned, the coroner summed up, remarking that there was considerable evidence that the intestines of the deceased had been perforated and the body considerably diseased. It would be for the jury to consider whether or not they thought the disease was sufficient to account for the perforation. Herapath's evidence that antimony had got into the system had been corroborated by Mr Moore, and the jury would have to consider whether this had anything to do with producing the perforation or causing her death.

The jury then retired. They had heard how Sarah Peters had died in agony after a painful illness over several months; how her doctor was not sure of the cause, and that then when traces of the poison antimony were found in the sample of urine taken before death he suspected that her death had been deliberately hastened; how an eminent toxicologist could find no trace of any poison in the body, even though he was certain that a substance had been at work; and how the cause of death was peritonitis caused by the escape of some contents through holes in the intestine. The breaches in the intestine could have been caused by a gross irritant, but they could also have resulted naturally from the consumptive disease from which Sarah Peters suffered. The jury were therefore faced with disease as being the most likely cause of death, but with a possibility that something more sinister had been used to expedite her demise. The only verdict they could safely deliver was that she died 'from a complication of disease accelerated by the presence of some irritant, but how or by whom administered there is no evidence before the jury to show.'

Silvester Peters was acquitted of murder, but the suspicion remained that he had been very fortunate. He seemed over-anxious to prove his innocence to the public at large, and towards the end of August, he released details of Dr Tomkyns's medical certificate for publication in the *Yeovil Times*. The doctor deprecated this publicity, and in September, he wrote to the *Western Flying Post* that he had signed the document on the understanding that it would not appear in the papers, 'but be kept for Mr Peters's own satisfaction'. It had merely revived a subject which must be painful to the widower, and which should have been allowed to rest. The 'highly respectable jury who investigated the case', he went on, had undoubtedly given their verdict conscientiously, but from the technical terminology used in the medical evidence, it would have been very difficult for non-professional persons to understand 'and fully appreciate the statements made by the medical gentlemen under examination'. In such cases, it would be advisable in future to have a jury composed entirely of medical men.

16

'NO ONE KNEW OF MY INTENTION'

Rode, 1860

In January 1829, Samuel Savill Kent, a factory inspector, married Mary Anne Windus, the daughter of a coach builder. They settled in Finsbury, London, and within a year, their first son Thomas was born, a sickly child who died soon after his first birthday. Two daughters, Mary Anne and Elizabeth, were followed by another son, Edward Windus. By then, the family had moved to the south west, settling first in Sidmouth. Edward was educated at Crewkerne, and at the age of 14, went to the naval school at Gosport. Six more children were born, the next four all dying before they were a year old. Mary's physical and mental health were beginning to decline by the time the last two arrived, Constance Emily in February 1844 and William Savill in July 1845.

In 1839, Mary Drewe Pratt, the 19-year-old daughter of a Devon grocer, became governess to the children. This lively, attractive girl probably presented temptations which Mr Kent, married to an ageing invalid who had borne him ten children, found hard to resist, but such gossip is difficult to substantiate. Factory inspectors were never popular, least of all with factory owners intent on cutting costs in order to increase their profits, and the relatively wealthy Mr Kent may have been the type of self-made man, always keen to better himself, with whom poorer members of the community were ready to find fault. Nevertheless, soon after William's birth, he moved out of his wife's room and into one next to that of the governess. He already had a reputation for being over-familiar with pretty maidservants, and soon stories were circulating throughout Sidmouth. After an interview with the local factory commissioner, he decided to move himself and his family away, and they settled at Walton in Gordano, near Clevedon.

Here, Mary Anne Kent found herself replaced as mistress of the house by Mary Pratt. The youngest daughter, Constance, was brought up mainly by the latter, and hardly knew her mother. After more local gossip made life uncomfortable again for the household, in March 1852, they moved to Baynton House, East Coulston, Wiltshire. Within a few weeks, family sickness had taken its toll. On 1 May, Mary Pratt returned to Devon to look after her ailing father; on the next day Mrs Kent was taken ill with stomach trouble, and died three days later. Mary hurried back to Baynton House and joined the rest of the family at the funeral on 11 May at East Coulston church. Four days later her father died. Wagging tongues suggested that the deaths might not have been due to natural causes.

On 11 August 1853 Mr Kent married Mary Pratt. In order to avoid further gossip, Mary had registered herself as a resident of the district of Lewisham, London, and the wedding took place there with Constance and her two elder sisters as bridesmaids. Their brother Edward was at sea at the time, and when he returned home on leave, he was so angry on being told the news that he left the house at once to rejoin his ship. Later he calmed down and accepted his stepmother as one of the family.

Back at Baynton House, in June 1854 Mary's first child was stillborn. Five months later Mr Kent heard that Edward had died when his ship *Kenilworth* was lost off the Crimean coast, a disaster from which there were thought to be no survivors. The Admiralty had no further information, though happily, a letter came from Edward a few weeks later, saying he had survived after all.

In the summer of 1855, a daughter, Mary Amelia was born. By then, Mr Kent found that persistent gossip about his past was proving a barrier to social acceptance, and Baynton House was too expensive to maintain, so he took a lease on Rode Hill House, near Frome. It was a large house with several spare rooms, though few members of the household slept separately. Sarah Kerslake, the cook, and Sarah Cox, the housemaid, shared a room, perhaps as Mrs Kent thought it wise to try and remove further temptation from her husband and forestall further grounds for gossip. Matters were complicated when the children took an aversion to their stepmother. Constance and William, the latter probably goaded on by the former, became so aggressive towards her that they were sent to boarding school in January 1856, but only for two terms, as their father could not afford to keep them there any longer. Twelve-year-old Constance refused to be educated by Mary any longer. One day, she persuaded William to join her in running away from home. She cut off her hair and dressed in some of his clothing, and then they walked ten miles to Bath and found lodgings overnight in a hotel. The suspicious proprietor questioned them and took William to the police station where he confessed everything.

Aware that the situation was becoming untenable, Mr Kent sent them back to boarding school, and ensured that Constance would rarely be able to come home for the holidays. Soon afterwards, he gained and lost a son. In August 1856, Francis Savill, known in the family as Savill, was born, and became the mother of his apple's eye. Just before his second birthday, the family learnt that Edward had succumbed to yellow fever on board his ship. Sometime that same year, 1858, another daughter, Evelina, was born.

In the interests of privacy, Mr Kent erected high fencing around his property. This, said his neighbours, suggested that Mr Kent, who had been suspected by some of killing his first wife, had something to hide. He also banned the locals from fishing along a length of stream on which he paid rent, something he was entitled to do but which only made him more enemies. This, and the nature of his job – which in some cases required him to order factories to suspend operations, and even lay off their workforce until certain basic health and safety practices were adopted – made him very unpopular in the district and beyond.

In the summer of 1860, as Mrs Kent was expecting a fourth child, tragedy struck. On the night of 29 June, Savill, a cheerful 3-year-old, was snatched from his cot as he slept.

There were then eight adults at home, including the youngest, Constance, then aged 16, and three children. Extensive questioning of everyone revealed nothing. Elizabeth Gough, who had been the Kents' nurse for eight months, said that Savill had been put to bed at about 8 p.m., and she herself went to bed at about 11 p.m. On waking six hours later, she noticed that he was not in his cot, and assumed that his mother had fetched him and taken him into her bed. This was unlikely, as he was too heavy for the pregnant mother to lift. Elizabeth went back to sleep, woke again an hour later, and knocked on the parents' door to check whether he was in there.

Once everybody was alerted, the house and grounds were searched, and it was found that the drawing room window was partly open. Everyone was surprised that Mr Kent appeared largely unconcerned, staying in bed instead of helping to join in the search. When he did dress and go downstairs, he said somebody must have stolen the child, and had his carriage prepared so that he could go and report it to the police at Trowbridge.

Although the family were unpopular in the village, plenty of people volunteered to help look for the boy. A labourer, Thomas Benger, searched the shrubbery and noticed blood around an outside earth privy. Lifting the lid, he found the body of little Savill in his nightshirt. He took it into the kitchen, and it was seen that his throat had been cut so savagely that his head was almost severed from his body. A piece of flannel was found nearby. When sent for, the laundress said she could not identify it as from any clothing which she washed for the family. Stephen Milett, a local butcher and police constable of Road, found a bloodstained copy of the *Morning Star*, a newspaper which the household did not take, and a small amount of blood on the privy floor.

Dr Joshua Parsons was called to examine the body, and at an inquest held at the Red Lion, he said that a sharp pointed knife had been used to stab the left side of the chest just below the nipple. There was also a blackened, bruised appearance around the mouth. For some reason this latter statement, though confirmed by several witnesses, was ignored by the coroner. He also said that he believed the child had been smothered by pressure of a soft substance over the mouth, but as he made that statement after he had been excused by the coroner, this was not entered on the deposition. The small amount of blood found where the body was deposited would have been consistent with death taking place before the mutilation of the body.

Sarah Cox, the housemaid, stated that one of her duties was to fasten the windows, shutters and doors at the front of the house before she went to bed at night. Mr and Mrs Kent had still been up when she went to bed on the night of 29 June, but she had still locked up as normal. The next morning just after 6 a.m., she found the drawing room door open and the shutters and windows slightly ajar. Mr Kent testified that he had checked the locks before going to bed and had found everything secure.

When he was asked who might have had reason for committing such a murder, he claimed that it must have been an act of revenge, either by someone in the village or by a former domestic servant who had a grudge against the family. At the time, the male staff consisted of a gardener-cum-coachman who had been with them for several years, and a boy who cleaned the knives and shoes and who was under notice to leave the following day. As they both slept out, neither was under suspicion.

The inquest was adjourned for police from Somerset and Wiltshire to investigate the case, as the town of Road (later Rode) was in Somerset, but Rode Hill House was (though no longer) just over the Wiltshire border. Sergeant Watts of the Somerset Constabulary found a bloodstained nightdress stuffed into a boiler, in an apparent attempt to burn it, and a bloodstained handprint was found on the window. Two Wiltshire policemen, Inspector Foley and Dallimore, passed over the evidence lightly on the grounds that the item had been shown to the police surgeon who said that the bloodstains came from natural causes. Later, the surgeon denied ever having seen it. The Wiltshire officers had ordered him to not be so insensitive, as it would only distress the family further. Foley allowed the garment to be returned to the boiler, and wiped the window clean himself, and the destruction of such vital evidence undoubtedly hampered the investigation.

When the inquest was resumed, members of the family, household and neighbours were questioned. The Revd Dr Peacock, a family friend and foreman of the jury, appealed successfully to the coroner for the pressure on family feelings and emotions to be brought to a speedy end, and a verdict of 'wilful murder by persons unknown' was returned. The locals were sure Samuel Kent was guilty, and thought that the Revd Peacock had manipulated the jury and coroner in order to protect him. There was pressure on Inspector Foley to arrest Mr Kent on suspicion of murder, but he could not believe that a member of the family would do such a thing, and he arrested Elizabeth Gough instead. As no evidence against her was forthcoming, she was soon released. Still the public clamoured for an arrest.

On 15 July, Inspector Jonathan Whicher of Scotland Yard was called in to lead the investigation, much to the dismay of Foley and the local force who resented his appearance. With a degree of determination which put them to shame, he proceeded to get in touch with and interview as many servants, past and present, as possible. From their answers, he soon discovered a history of resentment on the part of the elder children towards their stepmother and her children. Nobody, he soon understood, resented them more than Constance.

Esther Holly, the laundress, told him that Constance had gone to the laundry on the day Savill had disappeared, and asked her to fetch her nightgown as she had left a purse in the pocket. As she was about to do so, she was asked by someone else to get a glass of water instead. When the maid returned, Constance and the gown had disappeared. Although the maid thought nothing of it at the time, she later thought it seemed odd. If a nightgown had disappeared from the laundry room, Constance would be able to account for there being one less such garment in her wardrobe.

All this was enough for Inspector Whicher to arrest Constance, which he did on 20 July. She was remanded in custody at Devizes, and appeared before the court when the inquiry was resumed on 27 July. As there was no circumstantial evidence to convict her, she was released. Mr Edlin, a judge from the western circuit, solemnly told those present that 'if the murderer was never discovered, it would never be forgotten that this young lady had been dragged like a common felon to Devizes Gaol.'

Constance Kent, from a carte-de-visite photograph by J.E. Daniel, c. 1860. (© Mary Evans Picture Library)

Two days later, Mrs Kent gave birth prematurely to another son. At first it was rumoured that the baby had been born dead, though later reports confirmed that mother and child were doing well. On 10 August, a 30-year-old bricklayer, John Edmund Gagg, confessed to the murder and was remanded in custody. He said he had committed it for money, but 'never got any for it', and shortly afterwards asked, 'Do you think they can try Miss Constance again?' A searching enquiry was made before the magistrates, but it was established that he could not possibly be guilty and he was released. In October, Elizabeth Gough was arrested again, and released once more without charge. Meanwhile, a combination of gossip in Rode and the attention of the press made life so difficult for the rest of the Kent family that they moved again, first to Weston-super-Mare and then to Llangollen.

It seemed that the mystery might never be solved. When Rode Hill House was put on the market in April 1861, the press commented that 'as to the crime itself, we believe it is now given up as being among the things which are too mysterious to be inquired into.' Constance was sent to a convent in France at that time and stayed

Road (or Rode) Hill House, 1914 (© Nicola Sly)

there for two years. She returned to England in August 1863 and came to St Mary's Home for Female Penitents, Queen Square, Brighton. It was an institution mainly for unmarried mothers and prostitutes, and she entered as a probationer-nurse with, ironically, particular responsibility for newly-born children. She wanted to take Communion, and asked to be confirmed. The Revd Arthur Wagner, founder and director of the home, refused to accept her as a confirmant as he knew she was still under suspicion. This, he realised, would be an opportunity to establish the truth. Over three days of interviews with her in April 1865, he let her speak freely and she confessed to the murder of her half-brother. He took a written statement to send the Home Secretary, so she could be sent for trial. On 25 April 1865 she was taken to Bow Street magistrates' office. Attended by the Lady Superior of the home, and dressed in mourning, with a thick veil which almost hid her face from view, she confessed to Sir Thomas Henry, the chief magistrate, that she, 'alone and unaided,' murdered her half-brother. 'Before the deed was done,' she said, 'no one knew of my intention, nor afterwards of my guilt. No one assisted me in the crime, nor in the evasion of discovery.'

Some of those involved were shocked by her statement, but it came as no surprise to Inspector Whicher. He had always been convinced of her guilt, even to the extent of telling a colleague in confidence that nothing would be known for certain about the murder 'till Miss Constance Kent confesses.'

On 27 April, she appeared at the Petty Sessions court, Trowbridge. Wagner told the magistrates that he had not induced her to confess, and that she had done so of her own free will. She was remanded in custody at Devizes Gaol, and examined again in court on 4 May. The witnesses summoned included Dr Parsons, Inspector Whicher, Sergeant James Watts, and again Wagner, who said that Constance had entered the hospital as Emily Kent (Emily being her second name), so that people would be unlikely to connect her with the murder case. When questioned further, he said that all the communication he had had with her was made 'under the seal of confession', and he could not answer any question that would involve a breach of that secrecy. The chairman insisted he had to tell the truth, to which Wagner replied that his duty to God forbade him 'to divulge anything received in confession'.

Dressed in deep mourning and a thick veil, Constance was tried at Salisbury Assizes on 21 July 1865, pleading guilty to murder. As her written confession was read aloud, she broke down in tears, as did judge and jury. Mr Coleridge, QC, who appeared on her behalf, told the court that the prisoner wanted it to be known she was solely responsible for the crime, and that her father and Miss Gough, who had been suspected, were completely innocent. Contrary to speculation, she had not been driven to kill her half-brother due to unkind treatment at home, where she had had nothing but tender and forbearing love. The judge then spoke to Constance about allowing jealousy and anger to work in her breast, until they at last assumed over her the influence and power of the evil one, and she lifted the dark veil from her face as he donned the black cap and pronounced her guilty. In sentencing her to death, he added that as she was only aged 16 at the time of the murder, he was sure the sentence would be commuted to life imprisonment. On 23 August, the governor of Salisbury Gaol was informed by the clerk of the assize for the western court that Her Majesty The Queen had done so.

John Charles Bucknell, a senior physician, was asked to examine her and see whether there were grounds for supposing that she was mentally afflicted. With her permission, he wrote a letter to *The Times*, published on 28 August, revealing that Constance had told Mr Rodway, her solicitor, how she had taken a razor from a case in her father's wardrobe a few days before the murder and had hidden it. She had also hidden a candle and matches in a corner of the garden closet. After going to bed as usual on the night of 29 June, soon after midnight she went downstairs and opened the drawing room door and window shutters. She took the blanket from between the sheet and counterpane of her bed, placed it on the side of her brother's cot, and then carried the child downstairs and out through the drawing room. She was wearing her nightgown, and in the drawing room, she put on her galoshes. Holding the child in one arm, she opened the drawing room window and climbed out, going to the closet, lit the candle, and cut his throat as he lay asleep. At first there was no sign of blood, so she thrust the razor deeper into his throat, then bundled the body into the vault. The flannel found nearby was from an old garment in the waste bag that she had cut up to make washcloths for herself. Returning to her bedroom, she checked her nightdress, found two spots of blood on it and washed them out, then put it to dry and changed into a clean one. In the morning, the washed one was dry so she folded it and put it in the drawer with her clean clothes. Her nightdresses were examined by the police. A few days later, she held the nightdress up to the light, saw the stains were still visible, bundled it up and moved it several times before burning it in her bedroom and putting the ashes in the kitchen grate. She had cleaned the razor and replaced it in her father's bedroom during the confusion on the Saturday morning.

As for her relations in the family, at first she had liked her stepmother, but was keenly sensitive to anything that might have appeared as a slight towards her late mother. If she had heard any 'disparaging opinion', 'she treasured it up and [was] determined to revenge it.' She had borne no ill-will towards little Savill, other than that he was her stepmother's child, and declared that both her father and stepmother had always been kind to her personally. When Miss Gough was accused, she had made up her mind to confess if the nurse had been convicted, and she had also decided to take her own life if she herself was convicted. She had felt herself 'under the influence of the devil' before committing the murder, and had not said her prayers for a year before it had happened – and did not pray again until she came to Brighton.

Mr Bucknill said that her peculiar behaviour between the ages of twelve and seventeen, such as cutting off her hair, dressing in boy's clothes and planning to go abroad, could have been attributed 'to the then transition period of her life', and 'indicated a peculiarity of disposition' which suggested her future life 'would be remarkable', either for good or evil. He had found no sign of insanity at the time of his examination, and said it was impossible to ascertain the state of her mind at the time of the murder, but was sure that 'owing to the peculiarities of her constitution it is probable that under prolonged solitary confinement she would become insane.'

Had she been convicted in 1860, her life sentence would have meant fifteen years, or maybe she would have been released after twelve years with good behaviour. When she began her sentence in 1865, she was unaware that a 'life' sentence had been extended to twenty years. From 1877 onwards, she regularly petitioned the Home Secretary for release, arguing that conditions prevailing at the time of her crime should apply. After eight years of disappointment, on 18 July 1885, she was released from Millbank Prison on ticket of leave.

By then, her parents were long since dead. Her stepmother had succumbed to congestion of the lungs in August 1866, and her father to liver disease in 1872, aged about 78. Both were buried at Llangollen. William, who had changed his name to Savill-Kent, married in 1872. His first wife died in 1875 and he remarried later that year, and in 1884, they sailed for Tasmania, taking with them Mary Ann Amelia Kent, the oldest of Mary Drewe Kent's children. He returned to England briefly in 1885 and took Constance, who had now changed her name to Ruth Emily Kaye, back with him. In 1890, she left Tasmania and began a two-year training course for nurses at the Alfred Hospital, Melbourne. After several nursing posts, in 1910, she leased a house for nurses in Sydney and remained as its matron until she was 88, becoming resident there after her retirement. On her hundredth birthday in February 1944, she received telegrams from King George VI and Queen Elizabeth and the Lieutenant Governor of the State. She died two months later.

Another source suggests that Constance became mentally unhinged soon after her release, and moved to London where she retired to the sanctity or privacy of a convent. Yet another says she was a possible suspect in the Jack the Ripper murders, maybe even the perpetrator, 'Jill the Ripper', but this surely owes more to imagination than fact.

Whatever the truth of the matter, the case horrified Victorian England and has exerted its fascination on the public ever since. Between 1937 and 1947, three different plays about the murder were premièred on the London stage, and a television drama series was made and shown some thirty years later. All are indicative of recurring interest in a murder which concentrated minds perhaps more than any Somerset killing has done before or since.

17

'SPARE MY WIFE'

Dundry, 1861

In 1861, George and Sarah Waterman were living a peaceful retired life in a cottage in Dundry. George, aged 75, was a former soldier who had fought with the 9th Regiment of Foot in the Peninsula Campaign and had been presented with a Waterloo Medal with three bars for his service, of which he was immensely proud.

At first glance, the Watermans' retirement appeared relatively comfortable. They owned their cottage, and an acre of land, including an orchard. Neither George nor Sarah, then 73 years old, needed to work to support themselves in their old age, although George kept a cow and sold milk to the villagers. He was known to be careful with money and the couple lived simply, well within their means. Yet it was widely rumoured in the small village that large sums of money were secreted somewhere in the rather dilapidated cottage, and this was believed to have been the catalyst for the terrible events of Wednesday 9 January.

Between 6 p.m. and 7 p.m., they were sitting by the fire talking, while Sarah sewed. Their conversation was disturbed by a knock on their door. George asked the identity of the caller and was told that it was 'John, the Winford policeman'. Reassured, George opened the door to see two men standing on his doorstep, but before he could even begin to establish the purpose of their visit, one of them struck him hard on the forehead with a large stick. Dazed, he wandered back into the house, followed by the men who knocked him down and struck him about the head several times. When he regained his footing, they forced him upstairs, demanding to be shown where the money was kept. He protested that the only money in the house was in a box in the bedroom. They emptied the box, pocketing the 5 or 6s found inside, then ransacked the upstairs of the cottage, breaking open a chest of drawers and helping themselves to whatever took their fancy, including two old silver watches, a bottle of brandy and George's treasured campaign medal. At one point, they turned over the mattress in their search for money, and when they did, a brace of pistols fell to the floor. The intruders pointed the pistols at George and threatened to shoot him.

When they were satisfied that the legendary large amounts of cash were not to be found upstairs, they bundled George downstairs again and bound him hand and foot. They took him into the cottage pantry and tied him to the large bacon stand, instructing him to stay quiet for twenty minutes before calling his wife to free him. They then took some bread and bacon, which they wrapped in a handkerchief and left.

Dundry in the 1960s.

Throughout the attack, he had begged his attackers to 'spare my wife' but had been told by one of his assailants that she had been 'put to sleep'. Now, as he desperately called for Sarah, ominously there was no reply. He managed to free himself from his bindings and immediately went to look for Sarah. He found her lying unconscious on her side in the kitchen, in a large pool of blood.

Wrapping a handkerchief around his own profusely bleeding head wounds, he staggered outside and made his way to the cottage of his nearest neighbour, a butcher, William Lovell, who lived 150yds away. He arrived at Lovell's house at about 7.30 p.m., and told him that ruffians had murdered his 'missus' and nearly murdered him. Lovell rushed immediately to the Watermans' house, and entered the cottage to find Sarah lying on the kitchen floor as George had described. At this point, Sarah was still breathing, so Lovell carefully lifted her into a chair before going to the village inn to raise the alarm.

Within half an hour, Dundry-based surgeon, Mr John Shortland, had arrived at the cottage, where he found Sarah slumped unconscious in the chair, supported by two women from the village. On examining her, Shortland realised that she was very near death. The pupil of one eye was fully dilated and did not react to light, her pulse was weak and her breathing was heavy. He tried to administer a dose of medicinal brandy, but Sarah was incapable of swallowing, so he asked that she be taken upstairs and put to bed. Within half an hour, Sarah died from her injuries, and at the subsequent inquest, Shortland said they had resulted from four blows to the head. There were two deep cuts to her scalp, each about two inches long, and a large lump over the right eye. She had a fractured skull and had died as her traumatised brain had swollen following the attack. Shortland also examined George, whom he described as being 'in a very dangerous state from blows on the head.'

A telegram was sent to Thomas Waterman, the couple's nephew who farmed at Glastonbury. On his arrival at Dundry his uncle handed him a parcel containing a hundred sovereigns, the mythical nest egg, which had been concealed behind a stone in the house. At the same time, George's precious medal was also found.

Suspicion for the attack immediately fell on Charles and Matthew Wedmore, also nephews of the Watermans. Matthew was a labourer and waterman working in the Bristol quays, while Charles served as a private in the Marine Artillery, then stationed at Portsmouth. Charles Wedmore had visited Dundry the previous week while on leave from his duties, but had failed to return to his unit after his furlough ended. During his visit, he had called at the stable of The Revd G. Boutflower, asking a servant if he knew where Waterman lived. The parsonage gardener, John Keevil, had offered to show him and escorted him to George and Sarah's home. When they arrived, Keevil had knocked on the door and Sarah had called out to find out who was knocking. Keevil, the former police constable for the parishes of Dundry and Winford, had responded 'John, the old policeman.'

Sarah was alone in the cottage, her husband being at church. Keevil and Wedmore stayed for some time chatting to her, although she evidently did not recognise Wedmore as a relative. When they left, Keevil took Wedmore to meet his brother, William, who lived in Dundry. Charles Wedmore later went-to The Carpenter's Arms public house, where he became drunk and was taken back to his brother's house, staying there for a few days before going to Bristol.

After Charles's surprise visit, George Waterman discovered a cutlass missing from his home. In the company of Charles' brother, William, Waterman went to visit Charles in Bristol, retrieving the cutlass and exchanging a few sharp words with his nephew.

Charles and Matthew had both been drinking in the village alehouse on the night of the murder, and witnesses had seen them leaving the inn and walking towards the Watermans' cottage. John Keevil, otherwise known as 'John the policeman', had seen them near the cottage shortly before the murder was committed. Soon after, Sarah was killed by two men, one of whom closely fitted the description of Charles Wedmore, and who had visited a pub in Bristol and asked the landlord, Jeremiah Jordan, to pawn a watch for them. As a result, Charles and Matthew were arrested in Hotwell Road, Bristol, where they were lodging with Harriet Frances, described as a 'loose woman'. The arrest did not go smoothly, since both men were armed with the pistols taken from the Watermans' cottage and, while police struggled to subdue them, Charles fired a shot at a police officer. Fortunately, it missed its target, the bullet passing within an inch of the arresting officer, Sergeant Morce. A search of their lodgings revealed several items known to have been stolen in the robbery, including some bacon. Harriet Frances was also arrested, since the stolen goods were retrieved from her property.

The prisoners were taken to Clifton police station. Charles, the younger brother, was described as a powerful man of full stature, with a 'heavy, dull expression of countenance'. He had been drinking at the time of his arrest and was said to be 'wild and dissipated' in appearance. Matthew, known as Mat, was said to look as though he 'had suffered more of the wear and tear of life.' He was missing several

Dundry, 2006. (© Nicola Sly)

front teeth and had a 'haggard, repulsive aspect'. On the following morning, the prisoners were escorted to Bourton, after which they were moved to Dundry, where they were brought before George Waterman, who immediately identified them as his attackers.

Both Charles and Mat subsequently made statements, each implicating the other for Sarah's death. According to Charles, Matthew had been the one to strike both George and Sarah. Charles admitted only to stealing coins to the value of 11s 6d, a bottle of brandy and the bread and bacon. Mat disputed his brother's account. The robbery had been Charles's idea and he had been reluctant to accompany him. However, he had allowed himself to be persuaded and, while he admitted to striking George, it was his brother who had dealt the fatal blows to Sarah's head. Having found the pistols, Charles had been determined to 'blow the old man's brains out' but was dissuaded from doing so by Mat.

Their statements were taken as confessions of guilt and tallied with the account of the evening of 9 January given by George Waterman. The brothers were committed to trial by magistrates for the wilful murder of Sarah Waterman, and the proceedings opened in Taunton in March 1861. It emerged that Waterman had sold a house and garden to William, another Wedmore brother, about two weeks before the murder, and could have been expected to have had the proceeds of the sale still concealed at his cottage. This was thought to be the motive for the vicious attack on George and Sarah and, coupled with the identification by George of his attackers, the evidence of 'John, the policeman' and the discovery of items taken from the house in the possession of the Wedmore brothers, was sufficient for the jury to find both men guilty as charged. The presiding judge, Mr Baron Martin, sentenced them to death by hanging.

Until the moment the judge pronounced the death sentence, both brothers had treated their arrest and trial lightly, displaying a bravado that amounted to levity. The announcement of their fate was enough to wipe the smiles off their faces. In the days leading up to their execution, both brothers expressed remorse for the murder and were judged to have sincerely repented for their crimes.

They were executed at Taunton on 5 April 1861. Not having seen each other since their trial, their reunion in the gaol chapel was an emotional occasion. After Holy Communion, they were led to the gallows in a procession headed by the prison chaplain and the prison governor. Charles watched sadly as the hood was placed over Matthew's head and the rope was adjusted around his neck, and then it was his turn. They shook hands with executioner William Calcraft, and then the execution party withdrew. Watched by a crowd estimated at 7,000, the Wedmore brothers momentarily stood firm together on the gallows before the bolts were withdrawn and the platform fell suddenly from beneath their feet. Matthew died instantly, while Charles convulsed a few times before the hangman's noose claimed his life.

George Waterman eventually recovered from his injuries and went to live with his nephew Thomas Waterman. He died in South Molton, Devon, in 1877, aged 91.

18

A POLICEMAN'S LOT

Yeovil, 1862

In the small hours of Sunday 12 January 1862, drinkers were returning noisily home after an evening at the Railway Inn at the bottom of Hendford Hill, Yeovil. Constable William Hubbard of the Yeovil Police was going on duty, walking towards the Quicksilver Mail nearby. As he passed the crowd, he wished them goodnight, and as he had expected, was greeted with catcalls and abusive language. One of the men, George Hansford, tried to jostle Hubbard, but he refused to react and walked on.

A few yards further on, Hubbard heard a clatter of heavy objects on the road, followed by cheering. He turned round to see Hansford picking up a stone to throw at him. Though Hubbard had no time to duck, the drunken Hansford's aim was so poor that the stone fortunately missed its target. Hansford tried again several times but eventually decided he was wasting his time, and Hubbard continued up Hendford Hill where a colleague, Constable William Penny, was waiting for him.

Aged forty-one, Penny was a conscientious police officer. His career was probably all he had, for his family life was tragic. His wife had been committed to a lunatic asylum for several years, and their two small children, whom he adored, lived with relatives in Wincanton as he was unable to look after them himself.

Penny had heard the noise and had roughly seen what had happened. The man responsible for throwing stones, he had decided, must be arrested. Hubbard pointed out Hansford to him, and Penny stepped forward and placed his hand on Hansford's shoulder, asking him his name. Hansford replied with the false name of Sandle, whereupon Hubbard charged him with throwing stones and ordered him to accompany them to the Yeovil police station. Hansford denied the accusation and actively resisted. As the navvies began shouting and swearing at the officers, Penny realised that the situation was about to get out of control. He walked away, calling Hubbard to join him, and suggested quietly that it was pointless trying to take Hansford into custody because they were in such a confrontational mood. He suggested that they should return to the police station for help. They then hurried away, shouting at the men that they were going to Yeovil to get more men to take Hansford.

Sergeant Benjamin Keats, on duty in the town, had heard the noise and had already set out in that direction. As he began to climb the hill, he met the constables, and Penny asked for help to take Hansford into custody. The officers set off up the hill together to catch up with Hansford and his noisy companions.

By the time they had caught up with the crowd, they had reached the Red House Inn at the Barwick and East Coker crossroads. Hubbars pointed out Hansford, and Keats ordered him to be taken into custody. Again Hansford resisted, but Penny drew out a pair of handcuffs and managed to snap one on the man's right wrist. Hansford shouted for help, but only George Chant and Charles Rogers came to help, as the rest ran away.

Chant and Rogers decided to go on the attack. Rogers produced a stick and struck Penny a savage blow on his head, knocking him over onto the road, and then struck Keats on the back of his head, also knocking him over. Rogers next struck Hubbard and turned to flee. Hubbard quickly recovered his balance, and though blood was pouring down his face, he ran after Rogers, and a running fight ensued, which ended in Rogers being felled by a furious blow from Hubbard. Rogers realised that further resistance was useless, and begged the officers not to strike him again as Hubbard picked him up by his collar and marched him towards the Red House Inn.

Sergeant Keats had been temporarily stunned. As he came round, he saw William Penny lying on the ground being savagely beaten by Hansford and Chant. He shouted to Penny to get up and as he moved to help the fallen officer, the navvies stopped attacking him and took to their heels. Now fully recovered and full of fury, Keats charged after them and dragged down Hansford, who no longer had the energy to put up a fight. Chant continued to run and managed to get away. Returning with his prisoner, the sergeant was horrified at the condition of Penny and called to Hubbard for help.

On hearing the call, Hubbard released Rogers, who quickly slipped away, and ran to help his sergeant. Both men carried the badly beaten Penny into the inn where Mrs Rendall, the landlady, made him comfortable in her parlour. Blood was pouring from wounds on the injured policeman's head and Hubbard was dispatched to Yeovil for medical assistance. When Dr Garland arrived, he found Penny close to collapse, but a drop of brandy and water helped to revive him. Garland's examination revealed three deep cuts in the skull, his left ear was nearly severed and his head was badly bruised. There did not seem to be any fractures, and though Penny was sick several times, he appeared lucid enough and asked if he could return to his home to West Coker. The doctor thought it advisable for him not to move, and suggested that he should be put to bed at the inn for a while. Meanwhile, George Hansford was in the town gaol and George Chant was arrested in bed in his lodgings at Stoford. Only Charles Rogers remained unaccounted for.

When Dr Garland came to see Penny again the next day, the latter insisted he was well enough to return home, but the doctor told him to stay at the Red House for a few more days until he was better. Nevertheless, Penny disregarded the doctor's advice, and decided he would go home by cart that Monday afternoon. It was a decision he would not live long to regret. On 18 January, six days after the attack, he was dead.

On 21 January, an inquest was held in the New Inn at West Coker before the coroner, Dr Wybrants. After an account of the fight from the two surviving officers and medical evidence from Dr Garland, the jury returned a verdict of wilful murder against George Hansford, George Chant, and, in his absence,

The grave of PC Penny, Church of St Martin, West Coker. (© Nicola Sly)

Charles Rogers who had been identified as the third assailant. On 24 January, Hansford and Chant were brought before the town magistrates and charged with the assault and wilful murder of Constable Penny. They pleaded not guilty and were remanded in custody for trial at the forthcoming Spring Assizes.

Charles Rogers was captured on the next morning, 25 January, hiding in the stables of the Greyhound Inn at Dorchester. When arrested by Superintendent Pouncey of the Dorset Constabulary, he said he had hit Constable Hubbard because he was afraid that if he had not acted in self-defence, he would have been killed. Brought before the Yeovil magistrates later that day, he was similarly charged with assaulting the police and the wilful murder of William Penny. He pleaded not guilty and was remanded in custody to stand trial with his two companions.

Proceedings began on 31 March 1862 before the Hon. Sir Colin Blackburn, a Justice of the Queen's Bench, with Mr Cole and Mr Hooper leading for the Crown and Mr Ffooks defending. Mr Cole opened the case for the prosecution and Sergeant Keats and Constable Hubbard recounted the events of 12 January. Under cross-examination, Dr Garland stated that the cause of death was a fractured skull. In his opinion, although the fracture resulted from a blow by a blunt instrument, he believed that a handcuff was more likely to have caused the major injury rather than a stick. He also admitted that he did not discover the fracture until the post-mortem as fractures were difficult to diagnose. However, he was quick to refute the theory that Penny had inadvertently hastened his own death by leaving the Red House Inn against medical advice, saying that in his opinion, death had been inevitable.

For the defence, Mr Ffooks suggested that the stone throwing had not been of a serious or malicious nature, and that Constable Hubbard had neither warned the accused nor taken any action against those involved. As the original offence had been of a very minor nature, he did not believe that the constable had reason to feel threatened or in any danger. In addition, the constable did not attempt to make an arrest outside the inn until three quarters of an hour after the stones were thrown. During that time, he continued, the police officers had not been engaged in continual pursuit of the alleged culprit or culprits, nor had there been a continual apprehension of danger. This being the case, the police officers had no right to arrest Hansford, and therefore, the accused were justified in resisting what, to all intents, was an illegal arrest and in using any force they considered necessary.

The prosecution argued that the pursuit had never been abandoned. When the stones were thrown, Mr Cole stated, Constable Hubbard realised he was heavily outnumbered by his attackers and went to seek assistance, and as soon as he had found Constable Penny, he renewed the pursuit. At this stage the trial was adjourned for the day.

When proceedings were resumed next morning, Mr Ffooks stated that one of the main points they would have to ask themselves before reaching a verdict was whether any assault was committed by the prisoners in the first place when the stones were thrown. If there was no assault, then the police were acting 'in exaggeration of their duty' in attempting to arrest Hansford for a minor misdemeanour and for which they had no such right. If they had no lawful right of arrest, he believed the men were not guilty of murder but of justifiable homicide. If there was no intention to commit an assault when the stones were thrown at the constable, Ffooks maintained, then no assault was committed. There was surely no intention on the part of the prisoners to assault the policeman and they were merely going home. For a person to be responsible for a criminal act, there had to be an intention. In this case, he submitted, there was no such intention to assault the police or to cause reasonable apprehension of danger. With regard to the question of continual pursuit, he suggested that it was reasonable to infer that Constable Hubbard had hastened to the top of the hill after the stones were thrown not to get help, but because it was his duty to be there at midnight and he was late.

He considered that the police were determined to secure a conviction, and had thus been 'guilty of a great exaggeration'. The result was an unlawful aggression by the policemen upon the liberty of the three men. Who, he claimed, possessing the proud name of Englishmen, would not be provoked to resist? These men would deserve the scorn of everyone if they had not resisted, and it would be impossible, even for the most benign of philosophers, not to do so under such circumstances. The men had acted with great forbearance, and had refrained from exercising any unnecessary violence in defending their liberty. (Since when, one might ask, did wilfully throwing stones at a person without regard for the consequences not constitute 'unnecessary violence'?)

Mr Ffooks also made much of the fact that Chant had tried to take the stick away from Rogers to prevent him from causing any unnecessary harm. There had been 'no preconceived design' to commit violence, and therefore, in this case, the law of common intent did not apply. If the jury found Chant guilty of this serious offence on the basis of the testimony produced, it would be a verdict which would not meet with the approval of anyone who had heard the trial. He believed, with confidence, that when the jury had considered all the evidence, they would not feel justified in bringing a guilty verdict against Chant. As for Hansford and Rogers, Mr Ffooks stated that they had no weapon which could be termed deadly. They had merely 'used those weapons which nature had given them' to resist unlawful arrest, and nobody could have foreseen that in defending themselves, an innocent man would have been killed. Moreover, he went on, the police had a duty to the public to operate their powers with proper moderation. Penny's tragic death had come about by the foolish conduct of the police, and he was confident that the jury would not find the prisoners guilty of wilful murder.

Did Ffooks bear some grudge against the police? His veiled attack on their conduct that January night, and what seems his over-earnest defence of a drunken crowd ready to throw stones at the merest provocation, suggests that his views were rather heavily weighted against the guardians of law and order.

Nevertheless, in his summing up, the judge appeared to take a similarly liberal stance as he explained to the jury that there were many distinctions with respect to an arrest. A policeman had a right to arrest on suspicion of a felony, but in the less serious case of a misdemeanour, he had no such power to arrest purely on the suspicion of a misdemeanour having been committed. In the latter case, it was his duty to go to the magistrates and obtain a warrant. A policeman could only arrest for a misdemeanour if the offence was committed in his sight, on the spot and in fresh pursuit. It was regrettable that Constable Hubbard did not wait until the next day and then go to Yeovil magistrates to obtain a warrant. Had he done so, the judge went on, Constable Penny would probably still be alive. Unless the jury found these questions in favour of the prosecution, the capital part of the charge failed. So if the defendants were not guilty of murder, did they face a charge of manslaughter? The judge saw nothing in the evidence which would reduce the charge below that. In that case, how many of the defendants were guilty? With these questions, the jury were sent to consider their verdict.

After a long absence, the jury found George Hansford guilty of manslaughter, but with a recommendation of mercy on account of the police having exceeded their duty. Chant and Rogers were acquitted of manslaughter, but found guilty of assaulting Sergeant Keats and Constable Hubbard in the execution of their duty. The judge stated that in view of the verdict on Hansford, he would order the acquittal of Chant and Rogers, as the jury considered that the police had been over-zealous in trying to maintain law and order. Hansford was sentenced to four years' penal servitude.

Constable Penny was buried in the churchyard at West Coker on 22 January, with six of his colleagues bearing his coffin to its final resting place. A headstone, 'erected by some inhabitants of this Parish as a mark of their deep regret at his untimely end and also as a testimony of their great respect for a faithful public servant', paid tribute to the memory of the police officer who had died a few days after 'receiving severe injuries in the execution of his duty.'

19

'GOODNIGHT'

Ridgehill, 1883

Since the age of 9, Joseph Wedlake had lived with his aunt and uncle, Charles and Mercy Pearce, at their home in Ridgehill, near Winford. In 1882, aged 29, he was employed as his uncle's cowman. The Pearces had also fostered another child, their niece, Emma Pearce. She had come to her aunt and uncle when she was eleven, and now aged 21, she worked with her aunt in the farm dairy. At first, Joseph had treated Emma like a little sister, but as she matured into womanhood, his feelings had gradually changed and he had fallen in love. He did not voice his feelings, and it had never occurred to Emma that he might have had romantic inclinations towards her. She continued to see him as an older 'brother', while he worshipped her silently from afar.

She attended church at Winford every Sunday and Joseph would often escort her there but, in the late autumn of 1882, she became friendly with a local farmer's son from nearby Downside. Alfred Thatcher, aged 19, began to walk Emma home from church. Soon, the couple were officially courting, and Joseph seethed with jealousy as Alfred often stayed at the Pearces' farm after church for supper.

Joseph kept quietly in the background until shortly before Christmas. Then one night, as Emma and Alfred chatted at the farm gate, he approached them and thrust his lantern towards Alfred, saying; 'I've come to see whether you're good looking or no!' His gesture amused Alfred who asked, 'Don't you think we are?' to which Joseph grudgingly replied; 'There's not much the matter,' before walking away.

Outwardly, Joseph remained calm, acting in his normal brotherly way towards Emma, but inwardly he boiled with his jealousy of the good-looking man who he thought had stolen his girl. Over Christmas, he hatched a plan to rid himself of his love rival. He had no obvious quarrel with Alfred and believed that if he were to ambush and kill the young farmer, then he would not be suspected of the murder. He determined to lay in wait for Alfred as he walked home one night and fell him with the axe that was used on the farm to kill pigs.

Joseph bided his time until the ideal opportunity arose. Then on Sunday 7 January 1883, Emma and Alfred arrived home from church to find a friend, Bessie Marshall, sitting in the farm kitchen talking to Mr and Mrs Pearce. At 10 p.m., Emma and Alfred decided to walk Bessie home. It was a cold, foggy night and Joseph had kept himself hidden from view outside in the farm buildings. He watched surreptitiously as the three young people left, noting at the same time the appearance of a glow of light in his aunt and uncle's bedroom window, which suggested that they had retired for the night. He went back into the farmhouse for a lamp, and then noisily walked around the yard and stables settling the horses, making sure that his uncle could hear him going about his business. Next he went back indoors, climbing the stairs to his bedroom, again making enough noise to ensure that his uncle and aunt heard him go to his room. Once there, he took a large swig of whisky for Dutch courage, removed his boots and tiptoed silently downstairs again in his stockinged feet. Pausing only to grab the long coat that he shared with his uncle from a peg in the kitchen and to collect the pig axe from the cellar, he slipped outside and set off in pursuit of the three young people.

He soon caught up with them and overtook them, going unrecognised in the pitch darkness. Emma and Alfred left Bessie at Weaver's Farm and then set off home again. Hiding in a gateway in the darkness, Joseph saw another walker approaching and, as the man drew nearer, Joseph realised that it was Thomas, his younger brother. He asked Thomas if he had met anyone on the road and Thomas replied that he had passed three people near Weaver's Farm. 'That was Thatcher, our maid and Bessie Marshall' Joseph told him, adding, 'I'm going to kill Thatcher with the thing we kill the pigs with'.

Thomas assumed his brother was joking and laughingly told him to get off home to his bed, but Joseph insisted that he was going to kill Thatcher. Even though Thomas knew that Joseph was in love with Emma and was extremely jealous of Alfred, and even though he could smell alcohol on Joseph's breath, Thomas was unable to take his brother's threats seriously. The two walked together until Thomas turned to head for his father's house. As they parted company, Thomas was aware of a bulge in the back of Joseph's coat, as though something was concealed there and, just for a moment, he wondered if his brother's threats could actually be serious. He dismissed these thoughts and carried on with his journey home, leaving Joseph to head back alone towards the Pearces' farm.

Shortly afterwards, Joseph met another passer-by, whom he recognised as Charles Horler from Strode. Joseph pulled down his hat to conceal his face as the two men passed and Horler did not recognise him. However, he too spotted the ominous bulge at the back of Joseph's coat. Joseph stood in the lee of a bank, sipping whisky and waiting for Thatcher to say his goodnights to Emma and set off for home. Soon he heard footsteps coming towards him and, as the steps came level, Joseph stepped forward and swung the axe, saying 'Goodnight' as he did so.

The axe connected with a dull thud and, as soon as it did, Joseph realized, to his horror, that he had ambushed the wrong man. Mark Cox had been innocently walking to his work on the night shift at Winford Iron Ore and Redding Works when Joseph's axe had struck him a vicious blow between his left eye and ear, causing him to fall immediately to the ground, unconscious. Aghast, Joseph stared at the body on the ground. Then for reasons which he could never fathom, he swiftly delivered two more blows to the unconscious man's head, killing him instantly.

Back at the Pearces' farmhouse, Emma and Albert were still chatting quietly in the cosy kitchen. At around midnight, Albert heard a sound outside, quickly followed by creaking noises on the stairs and landing. He mentioned it to Emma, who laughingly assured him that the old house was always creaking, so he thought no more about it. The two sweethearts finally parted at around half past midnight, with Alfred walking peacefully home through the darkness to his father's farm. On his way, he passed the body of Mark Cox, but failed to spot it in the darkness.

It was not until the following morning that John Habberfield, a farm bailiff from Dundry, found Cox's body lying by the roadside. Habberfield alerted the police at Winford to his find, and Police Constable Orman was quickly dispatched to the scene of the crime. There he found Mark Cox lying on his back, his feet pointing towards Winford, his head towards Ridgehill. One hand was in his pocket, and the other lay on his breast. His hat, which lay beneath his head, was filled with blood. His flask and food basket were still slung across his shoulder. Word of the gruesome discovery spread quickly and soon villagers were flocking to the site to inspect the body. The spectators included both Joseph and Thomas Wedlake and, while Thomas noted nothing unusual about his brother's behaviour, he was surprised when Joseph begged him not to mention their meeting of the previous evening.

The body of Mark Cox was taken to his home, where two surgeons from Chew Magna, Mr Charles Collins and Mr W. Richardson Edmond, examined it. They noted the presence of three wounds on the deceased's head, caused by blows from a blunt instrument. The first wound extended some four inches from the left eyebrow towards the left ear and the skull beneath it was fractured. The second wound was a huge contusion above the left ear, again with a corresponding skull fracture, which the surgeons felt, would have occurred when the victim was already lying on the ground. The third blow had fractured Cox's jaw in two places.

Superintendent John Drewett of the Long Ashton police force took charge of the murder enquiry and suspicion soon fell on Job Wedlake, a second cousin of Thomas and Joseph. There was bad blood between Job and Mark Cox, stemming from an incident in which Job had allegedly shot some of Mark's pigeons. Numerous witnesses had heard Job say that, having been blamed for shooting the pigeons, he would make Cox 'suffer for it' if he were blamed again. He had also threatened to 'do for' Cox on numerous occasions. The discovery of what looked like clog prints in a field near the murder site seemed to strengthen the police's suspicions, since Job was known to wear clogs. At home, Job shared a bed with his 7-year-old brother, John, who distinctly remembered Job coming to bed on the night of the murder. According to John, he had woken once in the night and touched Job, so he knew he was still in bed. The rest of the family backed John's account, but even though his family swore that he had been at home throughout Sunday night, Job was arrested on suspicion of the murder and detained in the lock-up at Long Ashton.

At the inquest into Mark Cox's death, Superintendent Drewett said that enquiries were continuing into the murder and the inquest was adjourned. Soon, Thomas Wedlake was also taken into custody. Mark Cox was known to be afraid of both Job and Thomas and when a long mackintosh coat, owned by his father but often worn by Thomas, was examined and found to have traces of blood on the shoulder, Thomas joined his cousin in the Long Ashton lock-up. Again, his father Robert, with whom Thomas shared a bed, swore that Thomas had been at home all night.

Although police now had two suspects in custody, the evidence against both was flimsy. The families of both men could account for their presence at home at the time of the murder. The county analyst tested the blood on the coat, even though in those days it was impossible to distinguish between human and animal bloodstains, and stated that they appeared similar in appearance to human bloodstains. However, there was another very reasonable explanation for the condition of the coat. James Tovey, a butcher from Winford, had recently borrowed it and worn it while skinning a calf. Charles Horler, the man who had passed Joseph Wedlake on the night of the murder, was asked about his recollections of the coat that the man he had seen had been wearing. He testified that the two overcoats had looked quite similar in shape but that the mackintosh was of a different colour. Without more solid evidence, it was unlikely that magistrates would commit either Thomas or Job to trial for the murder.

Confined in the lock-up for a crime he did not commit, Thomas Wedlake grew ever more depressed. Finally, on 28 January, he asked to see Superintendent Drewett and, after being cautioned, made a statement implicating his brother, Joseph. Drewett went straight to the Pearces' farm, where he arrested Joseph Wedlake for the murder of Mark Cox. Joseph promptly blanched and burst into tears, crying noisily throughout the journey to Long Ashton police station. He remained silent as he was charged, making no comment about his guilt or innocence of the crime.

On the following day, Drewett returned to the farm and collected both the long coat worn by Joseph on the night of the murder and the pig axe. On 30 January, Jospeh Wedlake asked to speak to Drewett and informed him that Job Wedlake was the murderer. Drewett told Joseph that, due to an urgent appointment, he did not have enough time to take a formal written statement but that he would do so on his return. Four hours later, when Drewett went to his cell to take the statement, a sobbing Joseph had changed his story. Now he admitted to the killing, making his mark on a statement of confession written by the police officer.

Thomas and Job were promptly set free and magistrates subsequently committed Joseph to trial at the Somerset Assizes. Proceedings opened on 30 April 1883 at Taunton, with Baron Huddleston presiding. By now, Joseph had retracted his confession and was pleading not guilty to the murder of Mark Cox. In a state of near collapse, he sat weeping in the dock as the prosecution witnesses testified against him. There were no witnesses in his defence apart from his counsel, Mr Poole, who reminded the jury that it was not unheard of for people to make false confessions to crimes they had not committed. Joseph had no known quarrel with Cox, unlike both Job and Thomas, either or both of whom might have had more reason to commit the crime. In his summing up, the judge directed the jury that, if they believed that Joseph's hand had murdered Mark Cox, even if he was mistaken in choosing his victim, then their verdict must be guilty of wilful murder.

The jury took just fifteen minutes to find Joseph Wedlake guilty as charged and he was sentenced to death by hanging. In the days leading up to his execution, Wedlake showed great remorse for his crime. The rector of Winford, The Revd McTripp, made strenuous efforts to have Wedlake's death sentence overturned on the grounds of his previous good character and the fact that he bore no ill will towards Cox, whom he had killed in error. A petition for clemency was presented to the Home Secretary, but the appeal was denied. On Saturday 19 May, in the company of the murderer of Clara White (see Chapter 20), Joseph Wedlake was hung in a double execution at Taunton Gaol.

20

'YES, I DONE IT!'

Henstridge, 1883

On 28 March 1883, William Mullett was at home in his cottage in High Street, Henstridge. Just after 7 p.m., he was disturbed by a loud knocking at his front door. The caller was George White, enquiring about his wife, Clara, who had lodged with Mullett for the past five months, after the breakdown of her marriage of only a few weeks. Mullett was instantly wary. The last time George had called for Clara, he had taken her out and she had returned crying, with her clothing torn, claiming that he had beaten her. He was thus relieved to be able to tell George truthfully that his wife was not at home at the moment, having gone to fetch water from a nearby well.

George seemed in no hurry to leave. The two men chatted casually on the doorstep for a few minutes, with White asking Mullett about his new job working as a ganger on the Somerset and Dorset Railway and enquiring whether there might be a possibility of employment for him. Eventually, the two men strolled leisurely into the High Street and waited a few minutes more for Clara. When there was no sign of her, White bade Mullett good evening and walked off in the direction of Furze Lane, where the well was situated, 200yds from Mullett's home.

He obviously met Clara on the way as, when she returned to the cottage, she told Mullett that he had asked her to go for a walk. Changing her shawl for a warm jacket, Clara left her lodgings on High Street about 7.30 p.m.

Meanwhile, George was still walking slowly up the High Street, where he met two men outside the Wesleyan Chapel. Fred Gould and Robert Garland were passing the time of day when George ambled past, remarking that they seemed busy. Moments later, he returned and asked Fred, a former work colleague, if he might have a private word with him. Fred agreed and he and George stepped away from Garland into the chapel yard. There, George asked Fred to do something for him and, when Fred enquired as to the nature of the favour, George replied, 'I want you to pray for my soul.'

Fred advised George to pray for his own soul, asking why George had made such a strange request. George answered by telling Gould; 'Because I mean to do for her tonight!' Fred naturally asked who George was threatening to 'do', only to be told that the intended victim was Clara, George's estranged wife. At this, Fred angrily grasped George by his shirt collar and shook him, telling him that he had a good mind to fetch a policeman and that if George ever did such a thing, he would happily stand witness against him. George back-pedalled furiously as he laughed and assured Fred that he had not meant it, but was merely frustrated by his wife, who had written him four or five letters, which he had come to discuss with her. Smelling beer on White's breath, Fred advised him to go home and go to bed, which White promised to do as soon as he had seen Clara. By this time, Clara was standing nearby obviously waiting for her husband, so the two men parted company and Gould watched as the couple walked off together towards Henstridge Ash.

Minutes later, George and Clara went into the Bird in Hand public house in the village and George ordered a pint of beer. As he poured his drink into the glass, Clara was heard to comment on the fact that his hand was shaking so much that he was spilling and thus wasting his beer. The couple stayed in the pub for less than ten minutes, sitting quietly together and sharing the drink, which they left unfinished.

At 8 p.m., two young courting couples were walking home from Templecombe to Stallbridge. As they reached the top of Yenston Hill, they were aware of screams coming from the direction of Henstridge. At first they thought the noise was simply the sound of children playing, but as the screams grew ever more desperate, one of the young ladies expressed concern that something might be seriously wrong. As she did, a woman walking from Henstridge passed them on the road, saying nothing. Arthur Avis reassured his girlfriend Elizabeth that the woman would have spoken out had there been anything untoward happening. However, the dreadful screams continued and soon they were accompanied by the unmistakable sound of blows.

Through the darkness, Arthur could just make out two figures, a man and a woman, grappling on the side of the road. The woman was lying on the grass verge and, as Arthur and Elizabeth approached them, the man began kicking her. Arthur remonstrated with the man, only to be told that it was none of his business. As the man continued to kick the woman, Arthur shouted for the other young couple, who had fallen slightly behind, to come and help. Edwin Hann rushed up and called the man a drunken sot for beating the woman so viciously.

At this, the stranger stopped kicking his wife and approached the four young people menacingly. Again, he advised them to mind their own business, threatening that if they did not, then they would get a taste of the same medicine. Arthur and Edwin removed their coats and handed them to their girlfriends, to better be able to defend themselves. While the man was addressing her would-be rescuers, the woman had managed to drag herself unsteadily to her feet, something that seemed to enrage the aggressor, as he left the two young couples in order to knock her down again and continue kicking her.

Edwin Hann shouted that he was going to fetch the police, the announcement at which the woman cried out in desperation, 'Don't leave me! Don't leave me!' Arthur reassured her that he was not going anywhere, while Edwin set off to run towards Henstridge, leaving his friend to pelt the pugnacious stranger with stones, in the hope of distracting him from his murderous actions.

Meanwhile, three men walking towards Henstridge heard the commotion and ran to find out what all the noise was about. Seeing the man deliver a kick to the woman's head, Sergeant Major Charles Stanbrook of the Blackmoor Vale Troop of the Dorset Yeomanry leaped into action. He aimed his walking stick and dealt the man a powerful blow to the head, knocking him to the ground, where he was promptly seized and restrained by the sergeant major's two companions. Stanbrook then knelt down to assist the injured woman, lifting her head to see if she was breathing. As he did so, the woman died.

High Street, Hentstridge.

The incident had, by now, drawn a small crowd of spectators and Stanbrook took charge, as befitted a military man of his status. Having been told that the police had been summoned, he sent one man off to fetch a doctor and another for a cart to transport the dead woman to the village. Someone else sent for a lantern and when it arrived, the fighting man was quickly identified by local people as George White and the dead woman as his wife, Clara.

Police Constable Culliford arrived from Henstridge to find a crowd of around twenty people around the body, while Stanbrook and James Brockway were holding a man captive between them. The prisoner, who Culliford knew to be George White, was clutching his handkerchief to a bleeding head wound. The officer quickly handcuffed White and then searched him, finding a bloodied two-bladed clasp knife in his waistcoat pocket. He immediately cautioned White and charged him with the wilful murder of his wife, to which George responded almost cheerfully, 'Yes, I done it.'

Culliford escorted his prisoner to Wincanton police station, while his wife's body was loaded onto a cart and taken back to her lodgings. There Dr Robert Godolphin Long of Stallbridge carried out a post-mortem examination. Clara White was found to have a five-inch stab wound on the right side of her neck, which had severed her jugular vein. On the other side of her neck was a similar, slightly smaller wound and across the front of her throat, a deep abrasion, as though someone had tried to cut her throat from ear to ear. There was a large wound under her left eye and she had broken cheekbones and bruises all over her face and head, apparently caused by a blunt instrument. There were several wounds to the scalp, all between 3in and 6in long. Her lip was badly cut and her fruitless efforts to defend herself had left her hands and arms cut and heavily bruised, with a particularly deep cut on her right thumb that appeared to have been made by a knife. According to the doctor, Clara could either have died as a result of the numerous blows to her head, or because of blood loss from the slashed jugular vein. Long later examined the knife retrieved from White's pocket on his arrest and determined that it appeared to be stained with human blood and bore traces of human hair, matching that of Clara. He also examined White's bloody boots and concluded that kicking could have caused Clara's head wounds.

The inquest opened on the following Saturday. As George White stood observing the proceedings with his arms folded, looking bored and disinterested, the coroner's jury heard evidence from his former colleague, Fred Gould, who testified, as he had vowed to do, about the threats he had heard White make towards Clara. The police had traced the mysterious woman who had passed Avis and his girlfriend shortly before they had come upon the murder. Questioned as to why she had neither seen nor heard any part of the fight, Elizabeth Bulgin stated that she had passed a man standing at the place where the murder had been committed. She had not recognised White, nor seen any sign of a woman, it being a particularly dark night. The man had wished her goodnight as she walked by, and very soon afterwards, she had met the two young couples. As to hearing no screams or other indications of the dreadful events that were taking place, she admitted to being slightly deaf. Having heard the medical evidence presented by Dr Long, detailing Clara's appalling injuries, the coroner's jury decided that there was a case to answer against her husband for her wilful murder.

White appeared before magistrates at Wincanton on 2 April, where he was remanded to Shepton Mallet Prison to await the Spring Assizes at Taunton. His trial opened on 27 April 1883 and was presided over by Baron Huddleston. When the judge announced that White was charged with having wilfully and with malice aforethought murdered his wife Clara, White immediately pleaded guilty. A surprised Baron Huddleston asked the prisoner if he was fully aware of the implications of a guilty plea and the inevitable consequences that would follow his conviction. Twice White assured the judge that he fully understood the charges against him and that he wished to plead guilty. Huddleston sent for Mr Kitley, governor of the County Gaol and asked him to speak with the prisoner. Kitley took White to a private room outside the main court and explained White's position to him in great detail. However, when White returned to the dock and was again asked how he pleaded, he still replied 'Guilty.'

The judge could do nothing more than don his black cap and pronounce the death sentence on George White. On Monday 21 May 1883, in the company of Joseph Wedlake, who had killed a man in a fit of jealousy, White was hanged in a double execution at Taunton Gaol. It was his twenty-sixth birthday. He went quietly and calmly to the gallows, having seemingly accepted his fate.

It later emerged that strenuous efforts had been made to petition the Home Secretary for White's life. Clara White, it appeared, had been no saint. Although married to George for only a few weeks before their separation, as a result of her prolific sexual activities prior to her marriage, she had contracted syphilis, passing the disease onto George after their wedding. (It was also hinted that Clara's relationship with William Mullett was considerably more intimate than that of lodger and landlord.) Believing that he had married a woman of good moral character, George had become immensely depressed in the months prior to the murder, as well as suffering the devastating physical effects of the illness, which can include degeneration of the brain. In spite of receiving letters from the rector of Henstridge, supported by Dr Scallon of Milborne Port, who had been treating George for his illness, the Home Secretary saw no reason to issue a reprieve.

21

'YOU OUGHT TO BE HANGED'

Yeobridge, 1889

At about 8 a.m. on Wednesday 2 January 1889, Emma Jane Davies, aged 9, set out with a tin can from her cottage at Yeobridge, near South Petherton. Major Blake was a local landowner and George Davies was one of his employees. It had long been the major's practice to give milk to any member of families who worked for him and who were prepared to come and collect it, and Emma and her 11-year-old brother Arthur regularly used to visit his farm, a walk of about a mile, for the purpose. There was thick fog and heavy frost that morning, and when she did not return home, her mother became anxious. By mid-morning, she and Arthur decided to go out and look for her.

Soon after midday, Arthur was surprised to see two white stumps sticking out of a muddy ditch in Gore Field, about 60yds from the road. Surprise turned to horror as he went to investigate and realised it was his sister's body. Her clothes were disordered, a cord had been tied round her neck, she had been cut around the throat and several other parts of the body with a razor, and her dress was thrown over her head, which was almost severed from her body and forced into the mud. The state of the sides of the ditch suggested that she had struggled violently with her attacker. A doctor and a policeman were called. The milk can that the girl had been carrying was found under her body, its contents spilt across the path, and the can badly dented. Hair similar in colour to hers was found embedded in the base, and it was assumed that the can had been used to strike her. The razor was found nearby, with blood and mud smeared on it. Blood in the field suggested that she had been murdered there before her body was dumped in the ditch.

A man's footprints were discovered in the field, and carefully preserved in the hope that they might lead to identification of the offender. Dr Walter, of South Petherton, conducted a post-mortem examination of the body and concluded that the child had sustained several heavy blows to the head before her throat was cut.

There were no signs of sexual assault, and no motive for the crime could be established. Since several strangers had been noted in the neighbourhood in the weeks before the murder, it was assumed that one of them was responsible. On the night of 4 January, Samuel Reyland, a local labourer aged 23, was arrested on suspicion of the murder. Rejecting the idea of a stranger being the culprit, the police had immediately suspected him. He had absconded from the district about three years earlier to evade a charge of sexual assault on another young girl whose father worked for Major Blake. Only after he had gone did the parents agree not to press charges against him. He had returned to his father's house to work for his uncle, a road contractor at Martock, only three weeks or so before Emma Davies was killed.

There was no direct evidence linking him with the crime, but much circumstantial evidence. A local woman, Elizabeth Chant, had passed Gore Field at about 9.15 a.m. on the morning of the murder. She saw a man in the ditch, and when he noticed her looking in his direction, he tried to shield his face with a hat. Later that morning, she saw the same man walking across the fields towards Bower Hinton.

Further evidence came from a Mr Rockey. At about 9.30 a.m. that morning, Reyland had appeared at the nearby village of Bower Hinton, and joined Rockey in going to look for work. Reyland was perspiring heavily, and his boots were wet and muddy. Rockey thought this was a little strange, as it was so dry underfoot. When he drew attention to the state of Reyland's boots, the latter told him it was because he had just been to look after some tools he had left at Cartgate the previous day.

By the time both men stopped for refreshment at a public house, news of the discovery of Emma's body was spreading round the district. It was mentioned as they sat in the kitchen over their drinks, but Reyland did not react or make any comment. He did, however, show some irritation when the landlord's dog entered and started sniffing at his legs, and despite being driven away, kept on coming back until Reyland had to hold out his hand to keep it away from him.

When he returned home, his uncle, who had heard about the murder, asked him where he had been at the time. Reyland said he had been with a shepherd, Mr Wines, at the time. The man clearly did not trust his nephew, and went to the effort of checking with Wines, who denied having been with Reyland at the time. When he reproached his nephew, he added, 'Sam, this don't show very nice against you.' 'You don't think I'd do such a thing, do you?' Reyland retorted. 'Well, if you did, you ought to be hanged,' was the reply.

These factors were sufficient to secure his arrest. Dr H.J. Alford, the county analyst, examined the prisoner's clothing and, though unable to find any bloodstains, identified spots on the back of his hat as being milk, and a human hair in the collar of his coat, which was more likely to have been from the head of the victim than from Reyland himself. When an identity parade was held at the station, Mrs Chant picked him out from several others as being of similar height to a man she had spotted near the murder scene.

On 12 January, Reyland was charged at Ilminster Police Court with the wilful murder of Emma Davies. The prosecution was conducted by Mr J.C. Baker, and the defence by Mr H. Paull. Fifteen witnesses were called, and the case lasted nine hours. Mr Paull submitted that the evidence did not warrant the prisoner's committal, but the bench considered there was a prima facie case. Maintaining his innocence, Reyland was committed for trial, appearing at the Taunton Assizes before Mr Justice Wills on 20 February 1889.

During the two-day trial, the case for the prosecution was conducted by Mr Kinglake and Mr A. Wilson Fox, and Mr Metcalfe defended. There was an

Shepton Mallet Prison from the church tower, c. 1910.

apparent absence of motive. The only clue was a threat that the prisoner was said to have uttered when at Cardiff, that on his return home, he would be revenged on the little girl's father, though why he should have said this was never made clear. George Davies knew of no quarrel between himself and the prisoner's family. There were apparently several men called George Davies who were living, or had recently lived at South Petherton.

The lack of direct evidence was pointed out to the jury and they were warned against convicting on suspicion only. They deliberated for ninety minutes before returning a verdict of guilty. The rumour of a grudge was still circulated, and it was thought that owing to the state of her dress, there must have been some sexual motive, though none was ever established. Before he died, he wrote his family a letter confessing to the murder, and saying that he had done several irrational things since he was hit on the head with a lump of coal while working at Cardiff, and could offer no other explanation for his behaviour.

Reyland was executed by James Berry on 13 March 1889, the first man to be hanged at the then 200-year-old Shepton Mallet Prison.

22

'YOU WILL HAVE ME HERE FOR SOMETHING MORE SERIOUS THAN THIS'

North Petherton, 1913

On 3 January 1913, the people of North Petherton, going about their normal daily business, took little notice of the young man cycling through the village, with a parcel neatly wrapped in brown paper strapped to his bicycle. However, the dreadful scene that was shortly to be played out in the full view of many villagers, on the doorstep of a small cottage near to the church, subsequently captured everyone's attention.

The neatly kept cottage on the corner of Mill Street belonged to a respectable middle-aged couple, Mr and Mrs John Spiller. Both were at work, he as a mason's labourer and she as a launderess. The only people at home on that Friday morning were Mrs Spiller's daughter, Alice Atyeo and Alice's infant daughter, Frances, then aged about 20 months. Cyril Phillips drove the baker's cart through the village making deliveries for his employer, Mr Gadd, as he did every day. While the church clock chimed at precisely 11 a.m. he called at the Spillers' home and left the regular bread order with Alice. As he continued on his rounds, he had travelled barely 20yds further along the street when he heard a voice shouting, 'Hi! Hi!' Looking back, he noticed a man standing on the doorstep of the cottage he had just left and, thinking that the man wanted more bread, he indicated to him that he would be back in a minute.

Meanwhile, Mrs Elizabeth Strong, who lived in a cottage on the opposite side of Mill Street, happened to look out of her bedroom window. She saw the man appear on the doorstep and look up and down the street as if to see if anyone was about. The man then went back into the cottage, only to reappear moments later carrying young Frances Atyeo in his arms. As Elizabeth Strong watched, the man sat down on the doorstep, clasping the child tightly between his legs. To her horror, she heard the sound of a gun being fired.

Mrs Strong rushed downstairs and straight out of her front door, but as she approached the man and child, closely followed by another neighbour, Mrs Ellen

Sellick, another shot rang out. By the time the two women reached the doorstep, the man was sprawled backwards across the cottage threshold, the infant lying motionless between his legs with blood leaking slowly from a wound in her forehead.

Mrs Sellick picked up little Frances who was sadly beyond all help, her tiny mouth twitching slightly as she drew her last faltering breaths. Mrs Strong hurried off to summon the local policeman and doctor. PC Frederick Hilborne, who arrived within minutes of the shootings, found the man still alive but unresponsive, his eyes open and staring and his breathing laboured. With the assistance of a local baker, William Warren, the police constable picked up the injured man and carried him into the house. As the men went inside, the interior of the cottage seemed perfectly normal and undisturbed. The kettle was whistling on the fire and bread and butter had been placed on a table, as if in preparation for a meal. Then the two men discovered the still warm body of Alice Atyeo, sprawled face down in a pool of blood, her hair hanging loose down her back.

Dr C.F. Hawkins, who lived in the village, was also quickly on the scene. After a cursory examination of Alice Atyeo's body where it lay on the kitchen floor, he was unable to find a gunshot wound, giving his opinion that she had died from a broken neck. It was only at a later more detailed post-mortem examination that a bullet wound at the nape of the neck was found. Alice Atyeo had been shot from behind, the bullet having caused her neck to be broken. Hawkins also examined the man who, by this time, had been put to bed in a downstairs room. His pulse was weak and the doctor felt that he would not live for much longer. He eventually died at about 3 p.m. that afternoon, without ever regaining consciousness.

The man was Frank Atyeo, aged 26, the dead woman was his 21-year-old estranged wife and the little girl, their daughter. Atyeo had been born in Middlezoy and educated at the local school, where he was thought of as a steady, reliable, hard-working pupil whose cheerful ways endeared him to his teachers and fellow students alike. However, his sunny nature masked a fiery temper and he was always quick to remove his jacket and square up to anyone who slighted

The scene of the tragedy in North Petherton, 1913. (Mike Clapperton)

him, regardless of his or her relative age and size. His quick temper, coupled with his physical strength, gave rise to his nickname 'Lion', by which he was still generally known.

On leaving school, Atyeo secured a job as a farm worker. However, he was an ambitious young man and soon left his job to seek work in America. His stay there was short and he returned home briefly, only to go back to America again, before returning once more to Somerset. This time, when Atyeo came back, his sister was in service to Mr Merson, a local farmer and, while visiting her at her work, Atyeo met another servant working there, 19-year-old Alice Pleece. Alice gave Frank a reason to settle down. They were married at Middlezoy and their daughter was born on Alice's twentieth birthday. A good reference from his first employer, Mr Biddlecombe, enabled Frank to find work at Farringdon Farm in North Petherton and it was there that he lived with his wife and baby until November 1912.

On 4 November, Atyeo was convicted of drunkenness and assaulting a police officer, for which he was fined two small sums of money. Stubbornly, he refused to pay, and was sent to prison for twenty-one days. While in prison, he spoke with Superintendent William Williams, alleging that his wife was responsible for supplying the police with the information that had caused him to be imprisoned. Williams assured Atyeo that this was not the case, but Atyeo was unshakeable in his beliefs and also implied that his wife had been unfaithful to him. It was rumoured that Alice was pregnant again and that Frank doubted that the baby was his. 'After this is over,' he told the police officer, 'you will have me here for something more serious than this.'

Atyeo's imprisonment caused him to lose his job and with it, the tied cottage where he had lived with his new family for almost a year. Thus, in early December 1912, a few days before the end of her husband's sentence, Alice and the baby moved into the cottage in Mill Street with her mother and stepfather. Atyeo soon found another farm job on his release, but since it did not come with accommodation, he was forced to move back to live with his parents in Middlezoy.

The Atyeos' marriage had apparently been stormy for some time and Frank had often been heard to threaten his wife, although it was widely believed that these were empty threats, which he would never actually follow through. However, he had recently seemed on much friendlier terms with his estranged wife, visiting her frequently at her stepfather's home and regularly giving her money for the maintenance of herself and Frances. On the previous Saturday, it had even seemed as though the couple were considering reconciliation. Yet his father felt that he was depressed and Alice had complained to her stepfather that Frank had 'served her badly' since leaving prison and that he had even beaten her.

Those villagers who had seen Frank arriving at North Petherton on the morning of the tragedy were all of the opinion that the gun was newly purchased, since it appeared to be very neatly wrapped, as it would have been in a shop. A market gardener, Mr Richard West, had seen a young man, who he later identified as Frank Atyeo, attempting to buy a revolver from Charles Lane at his ironmongery in Bridgwater on the morning of the murders. Lane, who subsequently gave evidence at the inquest into the deaths, corroborated West's account. He had

Frank Atyeo.

asked to see Atyeo's gun licence before allowing him to purchase the weapon and Atyeo had promised to bring it into the shop on the following day. Asked why he wanted the gun, Atyeo had stated that he wanted to 'pop rabbits'. Lane refused to sell him the gun without first seeing a valid licence, so Atyeo had left the shop empty-handed.

He had not gone far. Shortly after 10 a.m. he entered Messrs Thompson Bros ironmongers and asked if they kept pistols. When told by shop assistant Arthur Taylor that they did not, he turned his attention to a rack of rifles, picking one up and asking the price. Atyeo protested that 19s 6d was too expensive, so he was shown a cheaper rifle costing 11s 6d, of the type commonly known as a 'garden gun', frequently sold to young people for target practice. Suitable only for killing small birds, it seemed far too innocent a weapon to be used for murder and thus required no gun licence. He spent a total of 12s on the small rifle and some cartridges.

North Petherton, c. 1920.

Taylor and Lane both described him as appearing calm and rational as he selected his murder weapon, and neither had any inkling of what he planned to do with it once purchased. However, it seemed that his actions on 3 January were definitely premeditated, since he had deliberately chosen a time when he knew that Alice's mother would be away at her part-time laundry job to make his fatal visit, and had purchased a weapon only shortly before carrying out the murders.

The coroner's inquest heard that the execution of Alice Atyeo and her child had been carried out extremely quickly and efficiently. Baker's boy Cyril Phillips had spoken to Alice on her doorstep and, while he had not seen any sign of Atyeo himself, he had noticed his bicycle propped against the side with a brown paper parcel tied to it and heard the child somewhere inside the cottage saying 'Daddy'. Before he had travelled 20yds further along the street, he had been hailed by Atyeo and turned to see him standing on the doorstep, by which time Atyeo had shot and killed his wife. Phillips had heard no shots, the sound of which had most probably been drowned by the rattle of the wheels of his cart, but within seconds, Atyeo had shot his daughter, reloaded his rifle and turned the weapon on himself.

The coroner's inquiry into the deaths lasted over two hours, although the jury needed only a few moments to deliberate before returning a verdict that Frank had wilfully murdered his wife Alice and their daughter Frances and then taken his own life. They found no evidence to indicate that he was 'out of his mind' at the time, leaving the coroner to pronounce a verdict of *Felo de se* – malicious self-murder – on Frank Atyeo.

A note was found in Atyeo's pocket after his death, written in his own handwriting. It read:

'There the tears of earth are dried,
There its [sic] written things are clear;
There the work of life is tried,
By a juster Judge than here.
Father in Thy gracious keeping,
Leave me now this servant sleeping'

Having read it to the jury at the inquest, the coroner remarked that it appeared to be an extract from the Bible or a hymn, and had no bearing on the case. Taken from a hymn written by John Ellerton in 1875, *Now the labourer's task is o'er*, traditionally sung at funeral services, it was probably intended by Atyeo to be his own epitaph.

Strangely, North Petherton had been the site of another similar incident only a few years earlier. In January 1897, Charles Tucker Roach cut the throats of his wife Elizabeth and 10-month-old daughter Jessy with a razor, before using the weapon to attempt suicide by slashing his own throat. Unlike Atyeo, Roach survived to be tried at Wells for the murder of his wife and daughter. He was found guilty but insane and detained during Her Majesty's pleasure.

23

'WHAT'S THE USE OF BAMBOOZLING ABOUT IT?'

Porlock, 1914

On 3 June 1914, having just shot his neighbour, 59-year-old Henry Pugsley, in the back, 55-year-old Henry Quartly calmly walked into his own house and went upstairs. There he turned his double-barrelled shotgun on himself, pulled the trigger – and missed. Meanwhile, Pugsley staggered into his home in Parson Street, Porlock, supported by his wife, Fanny. Minutes earlier, the couple, who were fruiterers and fish dealers, had returned from their regular delivery round on Exmoor. Fanny had gone indoors to make a cup of tea while her husband had stabled the pony, before walking the short distance from the stables back to his cottage. As he approached his gate, a shot rang out and Pugsley fell, bleeding heavily, his right lung peppered with shot. His wife rushed to his aid and was in time to hear his last words: 'I'm shot, mother.'

The fatal shooting was the climax of a long-running dispute between Quartly and the Pugsley family. In December of 1913, a case against Quartly had been brought before Dunster magistrates by complainant Mrs Fanny Pugsley. The charge against Quartly was that on 31 October that year, he had used indecent language within the hearing of the highway. According to Fanny, Quartly had entered her house where he had used foul and disgraceful language, an allegation that Quartly categorically denied. He maintained that Mrs Pugsley had been interfering with a tenant, Thomas Heard and, not for the first time, Heard had complained to Quartly, who had taken it upon himself to remonstrate with her.

The magistrates eventually dismissed the case due to lack of evidence, but that was not the end of the matter for Quartly. He brooded silently about the court case, becoming ever more antagonistic towards Mr and Mrs Pugsley as the weeks went by. The feud between them simmered on quietly until the summer of 1914 when Quartly received another summons to appear before Dunster magistrates on 5 June. Reluctant to make what he saw as another fruitless trip into Dunster, Quartly decided to take the matter into his own hands.

Like Pugsley, Quartly lived in Parson Street and his house had a garden some 12½yds from Pugsley's home. It was in this garden that Quartly concealed himself behind a 5ft high, flower-topped wall and waited for Pugsley, his shotgun at

Parson Street, Porlock. (© Nicola Sly)

the ready. Returning from his stables, Pugsley passed the garden and exchanged pleasantries with a neighbour, Mrs Chapman, who was standing outside in the street.

The street was quite busy. As well as Mrs Chapman, a young woman, Alice Middleton, stood nearby. Marmion Watts had just reached Pugsley's house in his horse and cart and John Bass's horse and cart was approaching from the opposite direction. Then, out of the blue, a shot suddenly rang out, disturbing the peaceful and neighbourly scene. Henry Pugsley immediately fell to the ground, slumping against his garden fence. Alice Middleton was winged by the shot and swooned; she too lay on the street. Watt's horse, startled by the sudden noise, was rearing and George Bushen and his wife Kitty, who had previously been taking tea in their nearby cottage, rushed outside to see what all the commotion was. All of them clearly saw Quartly hidden behind bushes in his garden. As Fanny Pugsley came outside to see what had happened, Quartly walked across the street and into his own house, closing the door behind him.

High Street, Porlock, 1960s.

A passer-by ran for the local police constable, and found him off duty and in plain clothes. Constable Joseph Greedy did not wait to change into his uniform but grabbed his handcuffs and ran to Parson Street. He arrived in time to see Mrs Pugsley helping her husband indoors and Alice Middleton still lying prone on the road. Before he could go to the assistance of either woman, a shot rang out from Quartly's home.

Constable Greedy rushed inside and hearing voices, went quietly upstairs, startling Quartly's sister, Emily, who was in one of the bedrooms. 'Look out, Mr Greedy, else he will shoot you too,' warned Emily, but Greedy did not hesitate. Spotting Quartly standing in a curtained alcove holding his gun, he leaped on him, pushing the gun from his hand and pinning him to the floor. His cries for help were answered by two men named Huish and Blackmore, who raced up the stairs and helped to subdue the prisoner long enough for Greedy to handcuff him. Only once Quartly was safely under arrest did the policeman notice the marks of Quartly's attempted suicide – traces of powder on his face, a bloody lip and a hole in the ceiling made by the shot.

Greedy did not wait to find out the condition of Pugsley and Alice Middleton, but took his captive straight to Dunster police station, where he was immediately charged with shooting with intent to kill. Quartly insisted that he had not intended to harm Alice but that his sole grievance was with 'Tacker' Pugsley, as Henry was known. In reply to the charge against him Quartly said philosophically 'I shot him, that is straight, that is the truth, so there is an end of it.' When Quartly was searched at the police station, his suicide note was found in his pocket. It read; 'I got no grievance against no one else only those two Pugsleys. They were the most dangerous crew I ever knew and have only got to thank themselves, as they started it.' [*sic*]

When it was discovered that Pugsley had died from his injuries, Quartly was immediately charged with his murder. Again, he admitted the shooting, asking only how long it had taken his victim to die and if the police were quite sure that he was indeed deceased. He was then taken to Exeter Gaol.

An inquest into Henry Pugsley's death was held a few days later. Told that he could attend if he wished, Quartly declined, saying that there was no point. The inquest was told that Pugsley had been shot in the back and that 117 shotgun pellets had lodged in his right lung. The coroner commended PC Greedy for his part in the arrest and he was later awarded the King's Police Medal for his gallantry. Robert Huish, who had rushed so swiftly to his aid, was awarded a guinea for his efforts. The inquest jury gave their verdict that Henry Quartly 'did feloniously, wilfully and with malice aforethought murder Henry Pugsley.'

Quartly was brought before Mr Justice Atkin at the Somerset Assizes in Wells on 20 October 1914. He refused to appoint a defence team, preferring to plead guilty and remain undefended, and the court case lasted less than nine minutes. Judge Atkins suggested several times to Quartly that he should plead not guilty and allow himself to be defended, but Quartly was adamant in his refusal. 'I know I am guilty' he insisted. 'What's the use of bamboozling about it? What's the use to go over it all again? I killed him and there's an end to it.'

In the face of such stubbornness, all the judge could do was to ask if Quartly had any further comments to make before sentence was passed. Quartly pulled out a piece of paper from his pocket and read his prepared statement; 'I shot him and I must expect to be killed. I can only die once. I fear no foe. I am leaving old friends behind me, but I hope to meet them all some day. I hope they will cheer up and keep up their pecker.'

The judge was left with no alternative but to put on his black cap and pronounce the death sentence. As he reminded the prisoner that he had shot Pugsley in the presence of his wife, Quartly sensationally interjected, 'I wish I had shot her, too!' The judge managed to complete his speech, after which Quartly was taken from the courtroom. As he left, he turned to the court and shouted cheerily, 'Well, goodbye all!'

Quartly was hanged by Thomas Pierrepoint on 10 November, in a new execution chamber recently erected at Shepton Mallet Gaol. A keen sportsman, lover of cricket and football, he had been a popular resident of Porlock, who, even on the morning of the murder, had been laughing and joking with regulars at The Royal Oak Inn where he enjoyed a drink. Pugsley had been equally well-liked, a local businessman described at his funeral as kind, industrious and genial. As the result of a petty quarrel, two decent, respectable gentlemen needlessly lost their lives in the most tragic of circumstances.

24

'GO ON, PUT DOWN WHAT YOU LIKE'

West Hatch, 1933

West Hatch in 1933 was a sleepy little village with a small shop and a school with sixty pupils of mixed ages, local children entering as infants and then progressing to the segregated junior section. At the age of 11, they sat scholarship examinations, and those who passed went on to secondary school. Those who failed or did not sit the exam stayed on until they were 14, when they were expected to find jobs.

Childhood in the 1930s was a time of innocence, yet one pupil who attended the small school at West Hatch at the time had a secret. Twelve-year-old Doris Winifred Brewer was pregnant. She was one of six children and her mother suffered from ill health. For the last five and a half years, Doris had lived with her grandparents in Slough Green, a home she also shared with her uncles, Herbert, Harold and Frederick Morse. Frederick, 32 years old at the time, was almost certainly the father of the baby his niece was expecting.

On Thursday 23 February 1933, Doris and Frederick were seen walking arm in arm towards nearby Curry Mallet, Morse pushing a bicycle with his free hand. It was a walk from which only one of them would return. Several hours later, Morse was found alone, soaking wet and weeping, by his brother Harold. Of Doris, there was no trace. According to Morse, he had last seen Doris walking towards a shed in a field adjacent to the River Rag. He had left her there, with a packet of crisps that he had bought earlier, while he went to check on some rabbit traps. When he returned three-quarters of an hour later, Doris was gone. Morse had searched the riverbanks, at one point even falling into the river, but could see no signs of her. As it began to get dark, he decided to make his way home to summon help, and on his way there he met his brother.

Police were alerted and search parties were immediately organised to hunt for the missing girl. It was bitterly cold and dark and the ground was covered with snow, so it was hardly surprising that she was not found until the following day, when her body was spotted lying fully clothed in the River Rag, in the parish of Curry Mallet.

A post-mortem carried out by Dr Godfrey Carter at Taunton revealed that Doris had died by drowning. Apart from two faint bruises, one on each cheekbone, there was nothing abnormal noted about the body, except for the fact that she was 'in a certain condition'. Approximately 4oz of food were found in the dead girl's stomach, which were sent for further analysis.

On the day that the body was found, Fred Morse accompanied police voluntarily to Taunton police station, where he made a long statement and was subsequently released. In his first statement he said that on the morning of the murder, he had gone to work as normal. After breakfast, he had met Doris by prior arrangement at a nearby crossroads. He had tried to persuade his niece to go to school and had even escorted her there, but at the school gates, Doris had begun to cry and refused to either go inside or go home to her grandparents' house.

Morse had told her that he was intending to go to Curry Mallet to collect some wires and rabbit traps. Doris had wanted to go with him, so he put her on the back of his bicycle. They had called at the Bell Inn at about 10.40 a.m., where he had purchased beer, cigarettes, two packets of crisps and half a pint of rum, receiving one penny change from the 8s that he had given to Winifred Crossman, the daughter of the licensee.

Morse had left his bicycle on wasteland. He had directed the girl towards a galvanised iron shed in a field, telling her to wait there for him while he checked his traps. Then, having given Doris a bag of crisps and her attaché case and also his watch for safekeeping, he left her at the field gate. He had watched for a few moments as she walked across the field towards the shed, but did not see her go in. When he returned about forty-five minutes later, the only signs he saw of Doris were her footprints in the snow and an empty crisp packet. He searched the area without finding her, falling into the river himself in the process, before deciding to return home and organise a search party. He passed witness Walter Woods at about 3.45 p.m., before meeting his brother shortly afterwards.

On the following Tuesday, Morse was escorted back to Taunton police station where he was detained overnight. At this point, he supposedly gave a second statement, contradicting his first. He later denied ever having made this second statement, claiming it was wholly fabricated by the police officers. The substance of the disputed second statement was that Morse had begun to have sexual relations with his niece some six months prior to her death. When he realised that she was pregnant, he and Doris had decided to commit suicide together by plunging into the river. The suicide pact had been largely Doris's idea, since she was frightened at the prospect of her mother's reaction to the news of her pregnancy. Accordingly, they had each drunk a quantity of rum before jumping together into the deep river backwash. However, once in the water, Morse had had second thoughts. He had managed to get Doris to the bank, but she had slipped and went underwater again. By this time he was feeling the effects of the extremely cold water and, having gone under twice himself, had barely managed to extricate himself from the river with the aid of an overhanging tree branch. He had been too weak to help his niece further, and was capable of little more than lying on the bank, coughing up water. By the time he had recovered, he was disorientated and unable to comprehend exactly what had happened.

After his second statement, he was charged by with the wilful murder of his niece by drowning her in a river at Curry Mallet, between 23 and 24 February. Morse had nothing to say in answer to the charge, referring Inspector Carter, who charged him, to the statement he had already made to Detective Inspector Bennett of Scotland Yard. He was remanded in custody at Exeter Prison.

The inquest for Doris was presided over by the coroner for West Somerset, Geoffrey Clarke. At the outset, Clarke asked if Morse was legally represented and was told that he was not. The coroner advised Morse to appoint legal representation for the forthcoming hearing, stating that it was beyond the power of a coroner's court to grant legal aid for this purpose. Although Morse was not called to give evidence, both of his statements were put to the court.

Several witnesses testified to having seen Morse walking arm in arm with the girl whom, they felt, seemed to want to go back in the opposite direction towards West Hatch. The couple stopped and talked several times as they walked through the village of Curry Mallett and, although the witnesses saw no signs of a struggle between them or any attempts by the girl to escape, the man seemed to be urging the reluctant girl to continue walking.

The coroner asked the jury to consider whether or not Morse was with his niece immediately prior to her death. How had she come to be in the river? Did she accidentally fall, or was she placed there, either by Morse or by another party? The jury decided that there was a case to answer, and Morse was remanded to appear before magistrates at Ilminster Police Court.

Much of the first session at the magistrates' court was taken up by ensuring adequate legal representation for the defendant. As he had not appointed counsel or a solicitor, due to lack of money, the magistrates granted him legal aid, the inquest being adjourned until 14 March, by which time a Taunton solicitor, Robert Young, had been retained to act for the defence. The second session concentrated largely on a review of the medical evidence, not just from Dr Carter, but also from the celebrated Home Office pathologist, Sir Bernard Spilsbury, who had carried out a second post-mortem examination on Doris's body on 1 March.

Carter testified that the body was that of an exceptionally well-developed girl who, physically, appeared much older than her actual twelve years. She had been fully dressed when found, wearing an outdoor coat and gum boots and, with the exception of one stocking, which was pulled down slightly below her knee, her clothing was undisturbed. He had found the girl to be in the advanced stages of pregnancy, actually in her eighth month. He had concluded that death was due to asphyxia as a result of drowning and had finished his examination by removing the contents of Doris's stomach, which he had sent for further analysis. The county analyst, Denys Wood, testified that the stomach contents smelled strongly of rum and were found to contain 4.3cc of 35 per cent alcohol.

Spilsbury then detailed the results of his own post-mortem examination. His findings corroborated those of Dr Carter and Denys Wood and he concluded that the analysis of the stomach contents suggested that Doris had drunk a 'fairly considerable quantity' of alcohol shortly before her death.

It fell to Mr Young, for the defence, to contest the evidence presented to the magistrates. He was quick to point out that his client vehemently denied engaging in sexual relations with his niece and fathering her child, and that there was absolutely no evidence to suggest that he had. He maintained that, had Morse pushed or pulled Doris into the river, there would have been some signs of a struggle on the riverbank, of which there were none. Finally, Young contested the validity of Morse's alleged second statement to the police.

Morse had always contended that the police had threatened and bullied him into signing the second statement, which they themselves had concocted. As part of their bullying, they had also invented a witness who had allegedly seen what had happened down by the river at Curry Mallet. Worn down by the constant pressure from the police, Morse had eventually told Detective Inspector Bennett, 'Go on, put down what you like', and then signed the statement just to get them to leave him alone. As Young pointed out, even though Morse was a poorly educated manual worker, his second statement was written without a single grammatical error. Naturally, Inspector Bennett denied all allegations of police misconduct relating to the second statement.

Young's eloquent defence of his client was in vain. The magistrates committed Frederick Morse to stand trial for the murder of his niece at the Somerset Assizes to be held in June. When formally charged, Morse responded, 'I plead not guilty. I have a complete defence and on my trial I will explain everything.'

The contentious second statement was the subject of lengthy argument at the opening of the trial, with Morse's counsel strongly questioning the admissibility of the so-called 'suicide pact' statement. Mr Caswell, now representing the accused, gained an admission from Inspector Bennett that he had been mistaken in stating that Morse had written the statement himself – he had simply signed it. Accusations were made that the police had bullied Morse, threatened him and lied to him. These accusations were denied by all the police officers concerned. As the presiding judge, Mr Justice Jeddard pointed out, if the allegations made against Inspector Bennett and Sergeant Salisbury, the officers from Scotland Yard, were true, then they were not fit to be members of the police force. It was suggested that the two officers had come from Scotland Yard to the country with the idea that the case must be cleared up quickly and that this had been accomplished without proper regard for the truth. The arguments continued back and forth, in the absence of the jury, before Jeddard finally ruled that he could see no reason to believe that the statement was not voluntary or that it had been obtained either by inducement or threat and it was thus presented as evidence to the jury.

The court heard from Doris's mother, Lily Brewer, who had been advised of her daughter's pregnancy less than a week before the murder. She had received a communication from local police officers, in which it had been suggested to her that she have her daughter medically examined. Less than three weeks before the murder, when Doris would have been in her seventh month of pregnancy, she had been taken to a local nurse, who had failed to discover her condition. On 17 February, a somewhat dissatisfied Mrs Brewer had taken her daughter to a doctor, this time obtaining the correct diagnosis.

Lily admitted that she had heard rumours about her daughter over the previous Christmas. She had questioned her brother, Fred, who had been most upset about her allegations. He had raised no objections to his niece being medically examined and had actually taken her to see the nurse himself.

Mrs Brewer was also questioned about her knowledge of the sleeping arrangements at her mother's home, denying that she was aware that Doris shared a room with her uncles, Herbert and Harold. She maintained that she had always believed that her daughter had had her own room.

On the second day of the trial, Morse himself entered the witness box. Having first described his various employments, he then went on to discuss Doris. She had lived with his parents since she was 7-years-old and he had often been responsible for plaiting her hair and preparing her school lunches. He again denied ever having a sexual relationship with his niece, claiming to have been shocked when he found out that she was pregnant. He also admitted that it had been he who had broken the news of her pregnancy to Doris on the night before she died. He initially stuck closely to the story he had related in his first statement and, when asked about the alcohol found in his niece's stomach, claimed that he had allowed her to take a sip of rum after she had complained of being thirsty. Far from the 'considerable quantity' of rum noted by Sir Bernard Spilsbury in the contents of the girl's stomach, he argued that Doris had drunk only about a tablespoonful.

Morse again contested the authenticity of his alleged second statement, which he still maintained had been a total fabrication by the police. He then dropped a bombshell by admitting that, while searching the riverbanks for Doris when she had first gone missing, he had actually found her body. Having searched for about two hours, he had found her lying on her back in the river. The water was just covering her face and she had drifted out of sight under some bushes. He had struggled to pick Doris up and onto the riverbank, but she had slipped from his arms. Eventually he had abandoned his efforts and dragged himself onto the bank, where he had consumed the remaining rum. Asked why he had not run to a nearby farm to get help, Morse stated that he had been too upset to think clearly. He had told no one about his grim discovery, as he had been too worried, particularly since his niece had been in his charge that day.

Under questioning from the counsel for the prosecution, Morse was unable to offer any explanation as to how his niece had ended up in the river. The jury chose to believe the evidence of the police officers over that of the accused and he was found guilty of the wilful murder of Doris Brewer and sentenced to death by hanging.

Morse appealed against his conviction, but it was dismissed. On 15 July, he petitioned the Home Secretary against his sentence but, having reviewed all the circumstances, the Secretary of State replied that he 'failed to find justification for asking His Majesty to interfere with the due course of the law'. With his last hope for clemency gone, Morse wrote to his mother from the condemned cell, asking that none of his relatives should visit him before he died.

Morse slept only fitfully on the eve of his execution at Horfield Prison, Bristol, but when told to dress himself, appeared outwardly calm. His only visitor, prison chaplain, the Revd Ivor Watson, chatted quietly to him as he waited to be escorted to the scaffold. At precisely 8 a.m. on 25 July 1933, Morse was handcuffed and led between two warders to the gallows, blindfolded and a few minutes later executed by Pierrepoint. His body was buried in a lime-lined grave within the prison grounds.

The day of his execution was a day of mixed emotions in the village of West Hatch. While the family of Frederick Morse grieved behind closed doors, the children from West Hatch School celebrated their annual charabanc outing to the seaside at Weston-super-Mare, leaving for their day out at almost exactly the same moment as Morse took his final walk to face the hangman's noose.

25

'I SHALL BE GLAD WHEN THE OLD BASTARD IS OUT OF THE WAY'

Bath, 1933

By 1932, Reginald Ivor Hinks had reached the age of 30 without having achieved much. He had been discharged from the army, dismissed from numerous jobs and had a history of petty crime. He moved from London to Bath, possibly with the idea of turning over a new leaf. For a while it seemed as though the move would be a good one for him. In 1933, he was offered employment by Hoover as a door-to-door vacuum cleaner salesman. While doing his rounds, he met Constance Ann Jeffries, a divorced woman and single mother, who was bringing up her 5-year-old daughter alone. He set out to woo Connie, they married after a whirlwind courtship, and he moved into the home that she and her daughter shared with her elderly father at Milton Avenue in Bath. He soon discovered that she was relatively well-off, having a £2,000 inheritance at her disposal. Her father, James Pullen, who was 81-years-old and had senile dementia, was also wealthy and owned numerous properties, in Bath and in Dorking, Surrey.

Within a short time, Hinks had embezzled nearly £1,000 from his father-in-law, part of which he used to move the family into a new home in Englishcombe Lane, Bath. Pullen was becoming increasingly frail, and at the time of the move, probably had very little time left to live. However, Hinks was impatient to get his hands on the old man's money – far too impatient to wait for the unfortunate Pullen to die a natural death.

Having dismissed the nurse who looked after James Pullen, Hinks personally took over his care and began a dedicated campaign to speed up the old man's demise. He took Pullen for walks and abandoned him in the busy city centre, hoping he would either be run over or succumb to the cold weather. On another occasion, Pullen was found wandering down a country lane, closely followed by Hinks in his car. When these attempts to hasten Pullen's death failed to work, Hinks apparently decided on more direct action. On 30 November 1933, he called police and an ambulance to the house on Englishcombe Lane. He explained that he had been helping the old man take a bath and had left him for just a moment to fetch some clean clothes. When he returned to the bathroom, he had found Pullen lying seemingly lifeless under the water, his face black. By the time the police reached the house, Pullen was sitting up in the bath looking remarkably healthy for a 'lifeless' man.

On the following night, emergency services were again called to the house on Englishcombe Lane where they were told that Pullen had gassed himself. They arrived to find the old man lying dead on the kitchen floor, partially dressed, with his head about a foot from the gas stove. His skin had the characteristic bright pink colouring of someone who had died from carbon monoxide poisoning. Yet it was noted by the attending doctor that there was no residual smell of gas in the kitchen, apart from a very faint odour emanating from the mouth of the deceased. On examination of the body, a bruise was found on the back of Pullen's head. In addition, the shelves had been removed from the gas oven and two overcoats draped over it to prevent gas from escaping. Was it possible that a man like Pullen, who suffered from senile dementia, would have been capable of planning and carrying out his own suicide? His doctors were of the opinion that he would not.

A post-mortem determined that the bruise on his head was very recent. According to Dr J.W. Heathcote, who performed the examination, it was consistent with Pullen either falling backwards and banging his head, or being struck. It was thought that the blow that caused the bruise would have stunned the old man, and rendered him both incapable of placing himself in the gas oven and unable to struggle if he was placed there by somebody else.

The inquest lasted several weeks as the coroner tried to unravel the mystery surrounding his demise. At the opening of the proceedings, the coroner advised Hinks that he need not answer any questions unless he specifically wished to do so. Nevertheless Hinks assured the coroner that he wanted to make a voluntary statement. He testified that Mr Pullen frequently fell and, in the fortnight leading up to his death, had suffered three falls. He explained that four months earlier, he had given up work to become a full-time carer for his father-in-law, and that he usually washed him twice a day, shaved him twice a week and gave him a weekly bath.

Mr Pullen, he said, had had a regular daily routine. He would eat breakfast, and then, weather permitting, sit outside on the lawn and listen to the wireless. According to Hinks, Pullen had threatened to commit suicide numerous times, either by cutting his throat, throwing himself in front of a train, jumping out of a window or drowning himself in a millpond. He had often said that he was tired of life and believed that he was a nuisance to his daughter. On the night before his death, Hinks said he had bathed Mr Pullen, shaved him and cut his toenails, then briefly left him in the bath while he fetched clean clothes for him. When he returned to the bathroom after an absence of only three minutes or so, it was to find Pullen submerged beneath the bath-water. He had dragged his father-in-law into a sitting position and pulled out the bath plug to drain the water, then called for his wife who brought towels, with which she began to massage her unconscious father's heart. There was no doubt in his mind, said Hinks, that Pullen had tried to get out of the bath and slipped, banging his head on the porcelain and knocking himself out.

On the day of his death, Pullen had risen as usual and come downstairs for breakfast. Although he normally dressed himself, on this occasion, he had simply donned a clean nightshirt and had refused to allow Hinks to put on his pants, vest and shirt. Hinks described Pullen's mood that day as 'extremely strong willed' and stated that he was also 'extremely tottery'. After eating a substantial breakfast, Pullen remained in the dining room with Hinks's stepdaughter, while Hinks and his wife washed up the breakfast dishes in the scullery. Soon the little girl came running in to her parents to tell them that her grandfather had taken a banana from the bowl on the sideboard. Almost immediately, Hinks heard a loud thump. Rushing into the dining room, he found Pullen lying on the floor, complaining that he had bumped his head.

Obviously confused, Pullen then decided to set off to walk to Dorking. He managed about 2 miles before he was picked up by Hinks and returned home in the car. After eating his lunch, he fell asleep in his armchair. The whole family took a short walk to the Co-operative stores in the afternoon, after which they ate tea, and Pullen again fell asleep in his chair. Mrs Hinks then went alone to the cinema, leaving her husband in charge of both her daughter and her father. Pullen woke up shortly before 6 p.m., declaring that he wanted to go for a walk but was told that it was too late. Half an hour later, he made another attempt to leave, this time saying that he was going to see 'his people'. Hinks told him he did not have any people and managed to persuade him to sit down in front of the fire again. However, twenty minutes later, Pullen went out of the room once more, this time saying he was going to the lavatory.

Soon afterwards, Pullen's stepdaughter called downstairs from her bed to say that her night-light was smoking, her feet were cold and she wanted a drink of water. Hinks filled a hot water bottle from the kettle on the fire, and then went into the kitchen to get a cup of cold water for the child. It was there that he found Pullen lying on the floor with his head in the gas oven. He pulled the old gentleman out by his ankles and attempted artificial respiration, before summoning assistance when he was unable to resuscitate the old man.

At the inquest, Hinks was questioned by the coroner about a cheque made payable to Pullen, the proceeds of which had been used to buy the house on Englishcombe Lane. Hinks explained that Pullen had owned some property in Dorking, including a shop that had been condemned by the Dorking Council. On the advice of his solicitor, Pullen had sold the shop, eventually receiving a cheque for the sum of £900. Pullen had endorsed the cheque to his daughter, Connie, who subsequently turned it over to Hinks. The money had been used to buy 'Wallasey', the house on Englishcombe Lane, some furniture and a car. Hinks asked innocently, 'There is nothing dishonest suggested about the cheque, is there?' and was promptly admonished for asking questions.

It emerged that the sale of the Dorking property was directly against the advice of Pullen's solicitor, Dr J.S. Carpenter, whose firm had prepared a new will for Pullen after his wife's death, with Mrs Hinks being named as the main beneficiary. However, in due course, Carpenter had become concerned that Pullen's money was being dissipated by Hinks and had taken steps to protect the estate by appointing a Committee in Lunacy. Having consulted with Pullen's doctor, Carpenter felt that the old man was incapable of understanding any financial transactions and had thus explained to Hinks that no steps could be taken to dispose of any property owned by Pullen. Hinks had assured him that he understood. However, in selling the Dorking property, he had bypassed Carpenter, instructing a new firm of solicitors in Dorking itself to handle the sale.

A witness was called who testified to having heard Hinks say, 'I shall be glad when the old bastard is out of the way. He is a damned nuisance.' The witness, a Mr Hiscock, alleged that Hinks owed him money for a wireless set and had promised to settle the debt on 2 December, which, as it turned out, was the day following Pullen's death. Hinks had sent Hiscock a postcard on 2 December, informing him that Pullen had died and promising to pay him £7 immediately after the funeral.

Pullen's nurse, Elizabeth Smith, dismissed by Hinks when he had taken over the care of his father-in-law, was also called to give evidence. She too spoke of the frequent suicide threats made by Pullen, of his tendencies to wander away from home and of his tearfulness on numerous occasions. She denied ever having heard Hinks swearing at Pullen. She described Pullen's mental state, saying that he was puzzled by the gas fire and would try to burn paper on it and poke it with fire irons. Pullen was unaware of his wife's death and often confused the nurse with his daughter. In Smith's opinion, Pullen would have been physically capable of turning on the gas taps unaided, had he wished to, although she was unsure as to whether he would have the mental capacity to plan and actually commit suicide by that means.

PC Ford, the police officer called to Englishcombe Lane on the night of the alleged suicide, told of taking a statement from Hinks after Pullen's body had been removed from the house. Ford told the inquest that Hinks had attempted to explain away the presence of the bruise in advance, saying that, if a bruise was found, then it was caused by Pullen's head hitting the floor when he was pulled from the oven. Hinks assured the police officer that Pullen had still been alive when he had found him. He had pulled him away from the oven by the ankles, turned off the gas, and then attempted to revive him by putting the hot water bottle he had just prepared for his stepdaughter on his heart and massaging the old man's chest.

Mrs Hinks was also called to give evidence before the corner. She too testified that her father had exhibited suicidal tendencies for many years and that he was

Englishcombe Lane, Bath. (© Nicola Sly)

prone to wandering off if not constantly supervised. She spoke of her marriage, saying that her husband had always treated her father with kindness, tact and patience. The strain of giving evidence for two and a half hours took its toll on Mrs Hinks, who fainted no less than five times in the witness box.

Having heard all the evidence, the coroner's jury took only twenty-five minutes to return a verdict of wilful murder against Hinks, at which he simply exclaimed, 'Well. What a shame.' He was immediately arrested.

His first appearance before magistrates in Bath was brief. Handcuffed to a policeman, he wept silently in the dock, as magistrates quickly dealt with a drunkard whose charges were also being heard that day. The drunk, a vagrant, was ordered to pay a fine of 10*s*, but could not pay and was sentenced to seven days in prison. On hearing this, three journalists present in court offered to pay the fine for him and the vagrant was promptly released. Then magistrates turned their attention to Hinks and, in less than three minutes, remanded him in custody for one week to enable the police to consult with the director of public prosecutions and for his application for legal aid to be considered.

After considering the evidence against him, magistrates subsequently committed Hinks to stand trial at the Old Bailey in London on a charge of wilfully murdering his father-in-law. In reply to the formal charge, Hinks said firmly; 'I have nothing to say and nothing to fear. Nothing at all – except that it is absurd.'

The trial opened at the Old Bailey on 5 March 1934, and consisted mainly of a repeat hearing of the witnesses and evidence already presented at length before the coroner at the inquest. However, there were some dramatic developments. One of these was an assertion by a Dr Fraser of Bristol that the bruise on Pullen's head could have been caused by his head hitting the floor when he was pulled from the gas oven by his ankles. Dr Fraser demonstrated the experiments that he had carried out which had enabled him to reach this conclusion by dropping a 7lb weight, which fell with a resounding bang, startling everyone in the courtroom. Yet in spite of Fraser's efforts, he was outnumbered. The other medical witnesses still argued that the bruising had occurred immediately before his death, probably deliberately inflicted by Hinks in order to stun the old man so that he could be placed in the gas oven without a struggle.

Hinks himself gave evidence in court for almost three and a half hours, during which he emphatically denied any wrongdoing in what he called the 'plain, deliberate case of suicide' of his father-in-law. At one stage, while being questioned about his resuscitation attempts on Pullen, Hinks protested in a loud voice, 'I don't wish to repeat the ghastly features of this suicide. It is more than I can stand. I can't go through all the ghastly movements of suicide and I won't. Neither will my wife.'

Yet the trial continued in spite of his protests and concluded on 10 March. Having heard all the evidence, the jury chose to believe that as a result of the post-mortem examination, the bruise on Pullen's head had been inflicted shortly before he had inhaled the gas, and that Hinks had dealt his father-in-law a blow in order to render him incapable of struggling as the so-called 'suicide' was carried out. They found Hinks guilty of murder and the presiding judge, Mister Justice Branson, passed the death sentence. He was executed at Bristol Prison by Thomas Pierrepoint on 3 May 1934.

26

'STOP WORRYING. IT IS ALL RIGHT'

Milborne Port, 1943

Ernest Digby enjoyed his service in the Royal Artillery during the Second World War. Known as something of a ladies' man, he relished the chance of meeting potential new conquests as his postings took him to different parts of the country. In 1941, he was stationed at Wakefield in Yorkshire where he met Olga Davy Hill. Aged 27, intelligent and ambitious, she worked as a local factory manager. She lived at home with her parents – until 35-year-old Sergeant Ernest Digby came into her life and swept her off her feet.

They soon formed a relationship, and Olga left her parents and set up home with Ernest in Wakefield. The relationship blossomed until, in March 1943, Olga broke the news to Ernest that he was to become a father. She probably expected him to do the decent thing and make an 'honest woman' of her, but there was an obstacle to her plans. A horrified Digby was forced to confess that he already had a wife. In October 1931, he had married Violet Thurley and they had three children, all living near London. He assured Olga that there was no longer any love between him and Violet, and that they stayed together only for the sake of the children. Then, to spare Olga the considerable embarrassment of giving birth to an illegitimate child, he somehow managed to talk her into marrying him bigamously. The ceremony took place in Canterbury.

By October, with the birth of his latest child imminent, Digby had been posted to Yeovil in Somerset. On 11 October, ten days before her expected confinement, 'Mrs Digby' arrived to join him, taking up lodgings in a rented room at Bazzleways Cottages in Milborne Port. A baby girl was born and named Dawn. Olga returned with Dawn to their rented room, but on 28 October, Ernest was transferred again, this time to Witney in Oxfordshire. Olga and the baby stayed at Bazzleways Cottages alone, until Ernest visited them on leave. He informed their landlady, Mrs Edith Gibbs, that they were intending to take the baby to his wife's mother in London. On 15 November, Gibbs watched as the couple left her home to walk towards the station, ostensibly to catch the London train. Hill carried baby Olga, while Digby carried two suitcases, but when they returned to their room that night, Digby was still carrying the cases and there was no sign of baby Dawn.

Mrs Gibbs was suspicious. It seemed inconceivable to her that a new mother would allow herself to be parted from such a young baby so, biding her time, she

Milborne Port station.

waited until the room was empty. On 18 November, she seized her chance and made a quick search. By this time, the smaller suitcase was enclosed in the larger one, surrounded by nappies, baby clothes and feeding bottles. Mrs Gibbs did not open the smaller suitcase, but the contents of the larger one convinced her that something was amiss. When Digby returned to Witney on 19 November, Mrs Gibbs went straight to the nearest police station with her concerns for the baby's safety.

In due course, Detective Inspector Dunn from Yeovil police station arrived at Mrs Gibbs's house to talk to Olga. Looking pale and exhausted, Olga insisted to the officer that her husband had taken the baby to visit her parents and gave an address in West Hampstead, London, where the baby might be found, living with her mother. However, when the police checked the address, there was no trace of either Ernest or baby Dawn. Olga was promptly arrested for child abandonment. During questioning at Yeovil, she tearfully told the police that she and her husband had taken the baby for a walk on 15 November. As they walked through a field in Milborne Port, he took the baby from her arms and told her to go on ahead. Distressed and confused, she said that she was struggling to remember exactly what had happened next. She did recall turning back to find that he no longer had the baby with him. When they returned to their rooms, he assured her that, while her back was turned, he had handed his daughter to a waiting nurse, with whom he had previously made arrangements to have the baby adopted.

Meanwhile, in searching the couple's room, police found a letter to Ernest in Olga's handwriting. 'There is no end to my worry,' the letter read. 'I am really tired of it all, heartaches and heartaches, and just cannot stand much more. If it were not for you, darling, I would join Dawn at once.' Asked what she meant by the phrase 'join Dawn at once', Olga blustered. She claimed to be confused and to not know what she was writing at the time.

High Street, Milborne Port.

By now Ernest had returned to his unit, which had moved to Witney in Oxfordshire. He was apprehended by two police officers from Scotland Yard and brought back to Yeovil for questioning, where he continued to insist that he had personally handed his baby to a nurse while out walking through the fields. He dismissed the contents of Olga's letter as 'confused nonsense'.

The police began to delve a little deeper into Ernest's background, and soon traced a Welsh girl to whom he had recently proposed marriage – omitting to mention the fact that there were already two Mrs Digbys. The long-suffering first Mrs Digby had also adopted another of his illegitimate children, whom she was currently raising as her own. She had seen Ernest only once in the past two years and, on that occasion, the sole purpose of his visit had been to ask for a divorce. There were also suggestions that Ernest and Olga had had another daughter together. Depending on who related the details of this earlier birth, the child had either been killed in an air raid, or was living with Olga's mother or her sister-in-law. She was certainly not living with her parents. A birth certificate for the first child, Doreen, born on 18 May 1942, was later found in Olga's possession.

After intensive questioning from the police, flaws began to appear in Ernest's story. Six hours into the police interview, he finally admitted that the adoption story was a lie. He and Olga had gone for their walk with the intention of abandoning the baby. They had deliberately chosen a field near the busy station, as they thought that the baby would be found and cared for. Ernest Digby was promptly charged with bigamy and child abandonment and held in custody at Yeovil police station while the police made further enquiries.

On examining Ernest's suitcase, they found that it smelled strongly of disinfectant. Next they interviewed some of his colleagues at Witney, where one soldier claimed to have seen Digby carrying a spade. Digby had an innocent explanation, claiming to have used it to clear some rubbish from his hut.

At this stage he was asked to make and sign a statement, in which he changed his story yet again. This time he claimed that he had tripped while carrying his daughter in the fields, and that the baby had fallen from his arms and cut her head. He had placed the baby, still alive, in his suitcase and hurried to catch up with Olga who was walking ahead. Later, with Olga again walking ahead of him, he had stopped to take the baby out of the suitcase, wrapped her head in nappies and left her in the woods. He and Olga had then gone to the cinema in Yeovil. After the film had ended, Ernest had gone back to the woods alone to find that the baby was dead. He had taken the tiny body back to his rooms in his suitcase – indeed, it had actually been in the smaller of the two suitcases when Mrs Gibbs had conducted her clandestine search of their room. On his return to his unit, he had taken the body with him to Oxfordshire, burying it in a large rabbit hole in woods near Witney.

Olga was also asked to give a statement. She claimed that her husband had hung back with the baby while the family walked in the fields near their home. When he caught up with her, he no longer carried the baby. She did not ask any questions about her daughter until later that evening, when she had begun crying and asked Ernest where she was. Ernest had reassured her, saying, 'Stop worrying. It is all right.'

Dawn's body was found where Digby admitted leaving it and returned to Yeovil for a post-mortem examination, conducted by Home Office pathologist, Professor J.M. Webster. This revealed that, far from being an accidental death as Ernest claimed, the baby had been struck violently on the head with something akin to a small hammer, pointed stone or a tree branch. The pathologist claimed that Dawn would have died from brain injury and shock within as little as two minutes. The police immediately charged both Olga and Ernest with murder.

They appeared together at the Somerset Assizes on 26 January 1944, where both pleaded not guilty to the murder of their daughter. Digby and Olga both testified at the hearing, maintaining that they had desperately wanted to keep their baby, who was described in the post-mortem report as well nourished and well cared for. However, they had found themselves in dire financial straits following her birth. Olga had been forced to give up her well-paid job on discovering that she was pregnant, while Ernest's army allowance was swallowed up in caring for his legal wife and their three children. Hence, they could see no alternative but to abandon the child.

Digby admitted to putting his injured baby into a suitcase, but maintained that he had only done so because he could not bear to see his infant daughter hurt and bleeding and because he did not think that Olga could cope with the sight. He stuck by his story of the baby being injured in an accidental fall from his arms and denied striking her, claiming to be surprised and shocked on returning to the woods where he had left the baby to find her dead.

Olga was close to fainting as she gave her evidence. She too asserted that she had wanted desperately to keep her baby but had been unable to see how they could cope financially with another mouth to feed. She claimed to have been too upset to question Digby once the baby had been left in the woods.

In summing up the case, Mr Laskey for the prosecution told the jury that if both Olga and Ernest had acted together in causing the death of their daughter,

North Street, Milborne Port, where Digby lodged. (© Nicola Sly)

then both were guilty of murder, even if Ernest alone had actually dealt the fatal blows to the child's skull. On the other hand, if the jury believed Digby's account and the child was accidentally injured, dying at a later stage when left in the woods, then he was guilty of manslaughter. If Olga had been a party to the abandonment of baby Dawn, even if she had not committed any violence towards her baby, then she too was guilty of manslaughter.

The jury deliberated for about forty minutes, before returning to court for further legal instructions. The foreman of the jury asked for clarification on the correct verdict for Olga, if they felt that Digby alone was guilty of the murder of Dawn. 'You must acquit her,' they were told by the judge, at which point, Digby was seen to lean towards Hill in the dock and whisper; 'You are all right.' Minutes later, Olga burst into tears and sank down on her chair as the foreman announced that the jury had found Digby guilty of murder. He watched as she was acquitted of all charges against her and half-carried out of the court by wardresses.

Asked if he had anything to say before sentence was passed on him, Digby addressed the court with only the slightest tremor in his voice. He thanked the court for the way in which proceedings had been conducted and also thanked the judge for his summing up of the case. However, he maintained that certain points had not been disclosed to the court.

Mr Justice Singleton then sentenced Digby to death by hanging, stating; 'This was a cruel murder for which I doubt any mercy can be extended.' Digby later appealed against his conviction, citing what he felt was an insufficient stressing of certain matters relating to the medical evidence in the judge's summary. However, the court of appeal found against him and Herbert Morrison, the Home Secretary, supported the post-sentencing comments of Mr Justice Singleton in denying a reprieve. Morrison's view was that, whether or not the murder was premeditated, Digby's rakish lifestyle precluded any consideration for mercy. He was hanged at Bristol Prison by executioners Pierrepoint and Wade, on 16 March 1944.

27

'THANK YOU'

Middlezoy, 1947

On 13 September 1947, regular drinkers at the George Inn in Middlezoy were unable to rouse the elderly landlady, Mrs Emily Bowers, at opening time. The pub's wooden shutters were still closed across the windows and a delivery of milk and newspapers was undisturbed on the doorstep. After repeated knocking on the front door brought no response, villagers went round to the rear, where they found the back door open. When their calls to Mrs Bowers went unanswered, the concerned local residents summoned the police.

Finding no trace of licensee Mrs Bowers on the ground floor of the pub, police officers went upstairs, where they found the 74-year-old woman lying dead on her bed, dressed only in her nightclothes. The room was in some disorder, with the blanket and an eiderdown from the bed lying on the floor. She had no apparent injuries, apart from two small scratches on her face and a bruise beneath her jaw on the right-hand side of her neck. A search of the premises revealed a broken pane of glass in a downstairs window, and what appeared to be a footprint on a windowsill and another on a shelf beneath it. The imprint of a stockinged foot was observed on the leather seat of a chair. A burnt-out candle stood on the bedside table, with two spent matches lying beside it, although no box of matches was found in the room.

The police were sure that Mrs Bowers had not died from natural causes, and immediately began inquiries into the circumstances of her demise. It emerged that she had last been seen alive by a neighbour at around midnight on the night of 11/12 September, when villagers returning from a trip to Windsor had alighted from their coach right outside the pub. At that time, she had been standing on the front doorstep, in conversation with two or three unidentified men who were standing on the step below her.

At a post-mortem examination of the dead woman, pathologist Mr Lewis formed the opinion that her death had been caused by heart failure and oedema of the lungs, brought on by over-exertion. The bruise on her neck was consistent with pressure marks where a hand or hands had tightly gripped it and the hyoid bone in her neck was fractured on one side.

An extensive search of the area around the pub produced a Vulcan matchbox, containing eight unused matches. Given that the matchbox lay about 100yds from the building, in the direction of a nearby Polish Resettlement Camp, and that many inhabitants of the camp had been regular patrons of the George Inn, police immediately began interviewing the men there, with the help of interpreters. Their attention soon focused on Staff Sergeant Eugenius Jurkiewicz, a man known to have previously visited the George Inn. He was taken to the police station at

The George Inn, Middlezoy. (© Nicola Sly)

Taunton where, through his interpreter, he voluntarily gave a statement admitting to having killed Mrs Bowers but denied intending to do so. He said he had first visited the George Inn some two weeks before the murder in the company of Mr Dewhurst, the English teacher employed at the settlement camp. Dewhurst had been persuaded to play the pub piano and the patrons of the pub had begun dancing. At one stage, Jurkiewicz had been partnered by Mrs Bowers who, he alleged, kissed him on the neck below one ear and stroked his hair.

On the evening of the murder, Jurkiewicz had been drinking with friends at a pub in Othery and had consumed five or six gins and four or five pints of beer. He confessed that whenever he drank alcohol, he became very excitable towards women. An hour after returning to the camp, he found himself in desperate need of female company. He went for a walk around outside and, while walking, noticed a light in one of the huts. Seeing a young woman inside, he tried to open a window, but the woman spotted him and shouted, at which he panicked and fled. Next, he went to another hut, in which he was aware that a married woman lived. He managed to climb into the darkened hut through the window, but on sparking his petrol lighter, saw that the woman was in bed with a man. When she awoke and challenged him, he ran away again.

Near the camp entrance, he heard voices, one of which he believed to be that of Mr Dewhurst. Knowing that he was a lodger at the George Inn, Jurkiewicz wondered if the pub was still open and, fuelled by his memory of what he saw as the tender moment he had shared with Mrs Bowers on his previous visit, he set off to find out. Finding the pub closed for the night, he first tried to enter the building by scrambling on top of the front porch and prising open the window. When this failed, he went to the rear of the pub and smashed the pane of glass, opened the window and climbed through it. He then made his way through the darkened pub to Mrs Bowers's bedroom, finding her asleep in her bed.

Not surprisingly, when Mrs Bowers awoke to find a strange man in her bedroom, she shouted in alarm, and Jurkiewicz quickly placed his hand over her mouth to quieten her. She refused to be silenced, turning her head away and shouted again for assistance. At this, he gripped her tightly around her throat. She struggled and he removed his hands from her neck, intending to leave. However, as soon as she was freed, she began to shout again, prompting Jurkiewicz to resume his grip on her throat.

Eventually she fell silent, and Jurkiewicz believed that she had made a decision to be quiet. Thinking that he should probably check on her, he tried to ignite his cigarette lighter, but was unable to raise more than a spark. Feeling around in the dark, he found the candle and matches on the bedside table and lit the candle, claiming to be horrified to see she was dead. After a cursory look round to see if he could find a glass of water or some eau-de-cologne with which to try and revive her, panic overwhelmed him and he fled back to the safety of the settlement camp, dropping the box of matches on his way.

Charged with feloniously breaking and entering the George Inn, and also with feloniously killing and murdering Emily Bowers, Jurkiewicz denied any prior intent to harm Mrs Bowers, claiming that he had only wanted her to be quiet. Tried for both offences at the Bristol Assizes on 25 and 26 November 1947, he maintained a military bearing in the dock as the evidence against him was put forward, never deviating from his initial statement to the police.

There was very little doubt in anyone's mind that he had committed the murder, although the defence revolved around his contention that it had been completely unintentional. The revelation that the defendant had spent two years of his life compulsorily seconded to a forced labour camp in Siberia evoked little sympathy from the jury, who needed only twenty-two minutes of deliberation before returning with a verdict of guilty of murder.

Lord Chief Justice Goddard asked the interpreter to inform Jurkiewicz that he had been found guilty, then, having donned the black cap, pronounced the death sentence. Only then did the defendant's demeanour falter, his face becoming drawn and his body slumping towards the front of the dock. As he was led away to the cells, he spoke just two words of English, saying 'Thank you' to one of his interpreters.

Jurkiewicz's death sentence subsequently went to appeal on the grounds that the jury should have been given the opportunity of returning a verdict of manslaughter. The Polish Army considered petitioning the then Home Secretary, Mr Chuter-Ede, for a reprieve of the sentence, and in Bridgwater, a petition was organised by local residents against the execution. However, all appeals and petitions failed and, shortly after his 35th birthday, Jurkiewicz was hanged at Horfield Prison, Bristol on 30 December 1947. His body was interred within the prison walls.

It was reported in the local paper that the contents of the George Inn were sold at public auction. Such was the interest in obtaining an artefact of the crime that the auctioneers allowed people upstairs to view items only a few at a time, for fear that the floor joists might give way. The police truncheon, which Mrs Bowers always kept within easy reach at the side of her bed, sold for 6s, while the bed in which she died achieved the princely sum of £6 10s. The successful bidder later told reporters that he would have been prepared to bid up to £200.

28
'ONE OF THE MOST TERRIBLE CASES OF MURDER I HAVE KNOWN'

Wembdon, Bridgwater, 1950

On Saturday 14 April 1950, farmer Geoffrey Moate of Wembdon, Bridgwater, looked out of his bedroom window at about 6 a.m. and spotted something unusual. Lying in the distant corner of a field, he saw something that he assumed was a sheep. He did not rush to investigate, but his 5-year-old son Richard did and soon came hurrying back to tell his father. Before Moate himself could take a closer look, the presence of the 'strange animal' had been noted by a couple arriving at the field shortly before 9 a.m. to milk their cows. Mr and Mrs Davey went straight to a nearby house and asked the occupants to dial 999 to report that they had found the battered and bruised body of a young woman.

Bridgwater police rushed to the scene and found the woman's body lying in the field, naked except for her shoes and one stocking. Scattered in the grass around her were a blue handbag, a flower-printed dress, a green tweed overcoat and the remnants of her torn underwear.

The body was soon identified as that of 26-year-old Lily Irene Palmer, an unemployed domestic and factory worker from Bridgwater. A post-mortem examination established that she had died from asphyxia caused by multiple injuries to her head and neck. Within hours, police enquiries had identified a likely suspect, Ronald Douglas Atwell, aged 24. He was arrested at his place of employment, the local gas works, and taken before a special sitting of the County Magistrates' Court that same evening, where he was charged with 'feloniously killing and murdering Lily Irene Palmer'. He was not required to plead. After two more brief appearances in court on 21 and 27 April, his case was formally adjourned until 16 May. He was tried for the murder at the Somerset Assizes at Wells, in June 1950.

The facts of the case were outlined in court. Palmer and Atwell had been out together for an evening's drinking at the Horse and Jockey Inn at Bridgwater, and after staying for an hour or so, left at about 9.30 p.m. Witnesses who saw them leave said they were both sober. Atwell was next seen alone by an acquaintance at about 1.45 a.m. in a lane near his home, and some twenty-five minutes later, at his house by his uncle, who testified that his nephew's demeanour at the time seemed quite normal. As the last known person to be seen with the deceased woman, Atwell was at the top of the list of those that the police wished to interview in connection with her murder. In his first statement, he admitted to having been drinking with Lily Palmer at the Horse and Jockey Inn on the night of her death. However, he told the police that he had briefly left the bar and gone into the pub's skittle alley and that when he returned, she had gone.

When the truth of his statement was challenged, he quickly changed his story. He admitted to having left the pub with Lily, saying that they had then walked together to the fields at Wembdon. There, according to Atwell, he had asked Lily to remove her clothes, which she had willingly done, and he partially undressed himself. He recalled that they had lain together on the grass for a couple of minutes and he had kissed her with the intention of making love to her, but had been unable to complete the act. Lily, he explained, had told him that earlier she had been for a walk with a Welshman and the thought of her being so recently intimate with another man had instantly banished any sexual desire he might previously have felt. At his failure, Lily had called him an offensive name and accused him of bringing her all that way for nothing. Atwell then stated that he must have 'gone off his nut'. He punched her hard on the nose, hit and kicked her and put his hands around her throat. He had finally come to his senses to find himself standing by what he soon realised was a dead body, checked her pulse and, finding none, returned home. There he noticed the following morning that his clothes were bloodstained, and he had meant to hand himself in to the police later that day, after he had finished work.

The prosecution disputed Atwell's account of the night of the murder. They advanced the theory that he had wanted Lily to undress but that she had resisted. At this, a sexually frustrated Atwell had engaged in a running fight with his victim, tearing off her clothes, punching and kicking her, dragging her face down across the field by pulling on a chain that she wore around her neck, and

Cornhill, Bridgwater.

stamping on her throat as she lay helpless on the ground. He denied this version of events, saying that he did not know how Lily's clothes had come to be torn.

Evidence was presented at the trial as to the mental states of both defendant and victim. Lily Palmer had been certified as 'mentally defective' three years prior to her murder. Atwell also had a lengthy history of mental illness.

His uncle testified that, as a small boy, Atwell was often uncontrollable and prone to displays of violent temper. Even as an adult, his behaviour was inclined to be childlike. Once, when his uncle had chastised him for taking money that had been put aside to pay a gas bill, he had cried like a baby. Another uncle and an aunt both told how he had been considered very backward at school. Every member of his family who gave evidence in court agreed that he had been badly affected by the deaths of both his grandmother and his girlfriend, after which he had become slovenly in his appearance and ceased to care about himself. When told by his uncles to 'buck himself up', he had simply cried. He had often arrived home the worse for drink, acting as if he were, as his aunt put it, 'dreamified'. On these occasions, she had been forced to shake him in order to bring him out of his stupor and had threatened him that if he did not give up drinking, he would have to leave home. He had also been discharged from the army for failing a mentality test.

Dr Charles Gibson, a senior physician at the Royal United Hospital in Bath, told the court that he had examined the defendant on three separate occasions and found him to be mentally unstable, although not certifiable. He was illegitimate and extremely sensitive about the circumstances of his birth. If he was insulted about his bastardy, he might snap and lose control of his actions.

At this point, presiding judge Mr Justice Oliver interjected to provide the jury with some direction on the law regarding insanity. He pointed out that it must first be established whether or not the accused was aware of what he was doing and, if so, whether or not he was aware that his actions were wrong. Dr Gibson then continued to say that it was possible that Atwell had been unaware of what he was doing at the time of the murder, that he had simply 'taken leave of his senses.'

In summing up for the jury, Mr Justice Oliver advised them that they must consider two facts of the case. The first of these was that medical evidence had shown that Lily Palmer had not engaged in sexual intercourse on the night of the murder, consensual or otherwise, thus the attack on her by Atwell could not be considered to be rape. The second was that the torn clothes contradicted Atwell's assertions that Lily had willingly stripped herself naked when asked, but instead suggested that her garments had been violently removed. The jury, the judge said, should ask themselves whether or not they had been satisfied by the defence's plea of insanity, since the burden of proof rested with the defence. He pointed out that, on the night of the murder, Atwell had returned home, knowing that he had left Lily lying dead in a field. Yet despite this terrible knowledge, he had still acted in a calm manner. Was this the calm of madness or the calm of callousness?

The jury took only ten minutes to decide that it had been the calm of callousness and to pronounce Atwell guilty of the murder of Lily Irene Palmer. 'This is one of the most terrible cases of murder I have known', opined Mr Justice Oliver, as he passed the mandatory death sentence on Atwell, who appeared unmoved in the dock as his execution was ordered. He died by the hangman's noose at Bristol Prison on 13 July 1950.

29

'THAT IS A FRAME-UP, THAT IS'

Bath, 1951/2

The murder of an innocent child is surely the most heinous crime of all and, in the 1950s, three little girls tragically lost their lives, seemingly to the same brutal killer. The culprit, John Straffen, escaped the death penalty as he was clearly suffering from severe mental illness when the offences were committed. More than fifty years later, he has now become Britain's longest serving prisoner. His lawyers maintain that his conviction is unsafe, since the judicial processes that convicted him were not valid.

Straffen was born in Hampshire in 1930. When he was 2-years-old, his father, a member of the armed forces, was posted to India and took the boy with him. While there, John contracted encephalitis, which left him with severe brain damage. The family returned to England in 1938, and took up residence over a café in Bath.

Straffen's childhood was a troubled one. He regularly played truant from school, and before his 10th birthday, he had been cautioned by the police twice for stealing; the first time a rabbit, the second, a comic. When he subsequently stole a purse, he was taken before Bath Juvenile Court and sentenced to twelve months probation. A breach of his conditions saw him brought before magistrates again in 1940. Before appearing in court, he had been examined by his school medical officer who certified him as a 'mental defective', and he was sent to an institute for mentally defective children. He spent the next six years institutionalised at schools in Warwickshire and Worcestershire, before being permitted to leave on 31 March 1946. However, once freed, he was soon in trouble again.

In 1947, he assaulted a 13-year-old girl in Bathwick, who fortunately escaped physically unharmed. On that occasion, the police took no action. Next he was arrested for theft, although the stolen goods were recovered, since he promptly told the police exactly where he had hidden them. Finally, on 12 September, an argument with a girl caused him to fly into a rage and, in his temper, he wrung the necks of several chickens belonging to his father.

He was committed to Horfield Prison in Bristol, where doctors examined him again. They reached the same conclusions as his school medical officer; Straffen was officially certified as being a 'feeble-minded person' and sent to a colony for mental defectives at Almondsbury. He escaped twice, before finally being released on licence to his parents in 1949, finding work as a labourer for a market gardener shortly afterwards. As a condition of his licence, Straffen was medically examined at Bristol Hospital, where doctors discovered the extensive brain damage caused by his childhood bout of encephalitis. Nevertheless, they did not revoke his licence, and on 15 July 1951, he committed his first murder.

Six-year-old Brenda Goddard was the only surviving child of a young widow, who was forced to work in order to support herself and her daughter, who lived with foster-parents in Camden Crescent, Bath. She had left her home shortly after eating Sunday lunch, even though she was expected to get ready for Sunday school, which she attended every week. Her guardians, Doris and Arthur Pullen, began an immediate search and her disappearance was reported to the police at 3.30 p.m. Her body was discovered at around 7 p.m. in a densely wooded copse behind Camden Crescent, known to local children as 'The Private'. She had been strangled. A later post-mortem examination placed the time of her death at between 2.30 and 3 p.m.

Police began extensive house-to-house enquiries in the area and, on the following day, requested the assistance of officers from Scotland Yard who arrived on Tuesday morning. It was believed that someone local to Camden Crescent had committed the murder, since few outsiders were aware of the existence of 'The Private'. In addition, Brenda was described as a timid child who would have run away if approached by a stranger. Enquiries focused on several mysterious men seen in the area around the time of her disappearance. One, described by witnesses as 'frightened and agitated', had purchased a pint of stout at a local bar on the evening of the child's murder. Another stranger had been given a lift from Bournemouth to Bath by a coach party returning to the area and a third man had been seen, in an obvious hurry, climbing over a wall at the back of Camden Crescent.

Camden Crescent, Bath. (© Nicola Sly)

Meanwhile, Brenda's foster parents received an anonymous letter, posted from Birmingham to their home at 'SUMERSET' [sic]. Written in pencil and signed 'Yours truly, H.R.G.', the letter expressed the writer's great sorrow for 'what I did to your daughter'. It promised that the writer's body would be found somewhere within the next two weeks but also ominously hinted that, within the same period of time, there might be another murder. A handwriting expert was called in to examine the letter and suggested that it was most probably written by a left-handed elderly person, possibly a woman.

While she had been out searching for her foster-daughter, Mrs Pullen recalled seeing a man who she described as aged about 35 and wearing a navy blue suit, walking near where the body was found. The police continued to interview local men and, on 31 July, it was Straffen's turn to be questioned. He admitted to being in the area at the time of the murder, to having worn a navy suit, and to walking in the woods where the body had been found. However, he maintained that he had not come forward in response to widely publicised police appeals because the man being sought in connection with the murder was aged 35 and he was only 21 years old. Police could find no evidence to connect Straffen to the murder and had to release him. He was subsequently questioned for a second time and released again.

On Wednesday 8 August 1951, Straffen went to the Forum cinema in Bath to see *Tarzan and the Jungle Queen*. There, he befriended a 9-year-old girl, Cicely Batstone, who had been allowed to go to the cinema on her own as a special treat. When the film finished, Straffen asked Cicely if she wanted to see another one. He persuaded her to accompany him to the Scala cinema, which was showing *She Wore a Yellow Ribbon*. After the film had finished, he took Cicely to a nearby field and strangled her, again with his bare hands. Leaving her body under a hedge in the field, he bought himself a bag of chips and went home.

Cicely's parents had been out for the evening, safe in the knowledge that their elder daughter, Gladys, would look after Cicely when she returned from the cinema. However, when Gladys arrived home from work to find Cicely was not at home, she assumed that her sister was with their parents and went to Bristol for the evening. Mr and Mrs Batstone got back to find the house empty and a note from Gladys to say that she had gone to Bristol. They presumed that Cicely had accompanied Gladys and it was not until Gladys arrived home alone at around 11 p.m. that they realised Cicely was missing and telephoned the police. An immediate search was launched for the missing child and her body was found in the field, known locally as 'The Tumps' at 8.30 a.m. the next day. Soon afterwards, the police were on Straffen's doorstep.

His journey to the cinema with Cicely had involved a bus ride and the conductor knew him as an ex-work colleague. He recalled Straffen being accompanied on his journey by a little girl, whom he later identified from photographs as Cicely. Another witness, Mrs Spencer, who also knew Straffen, had seen him with the girl. A courting couple came forward to say that they had seen Straffen and Cicely lying down in the field. A further witness, Mrs Cowley, was the wife of a police officer. When Mrs Cowley's husband was urgently called from home to work on the case, it was because of her ability to pinpoint the time and place where she had seen Straffen and the girl so precisely that Cicely's body was so quickly discovered.

The Tumps, Bath. (©Nicola Sly)

Asked to accompany police officers for questioning, Straffen asked, 'Is it about that little girl I went to the pictures with last night?' He then described the previous evening in detail to the police, telling them that he had left the girl asleep under the hedge. Later that day, Straffen approached a police sergeant and offered to show him how he 'did' the first girl. He then went on to explain exactly how he had squeezed Brenda Goddard's neck and hit her head against a wall until she was dead. Her murder had, according to Straffen, taken just a couple of minutes and he had felt nothing afterwards.

Straffen was charged with the murders of both Brenda Goddard and Cicely Batstone and he was committed for trial at Taunton. When his case opened on 17 October, the only witness called to testify was the medical officer from Bristol Prison, Dr Parks, who told the court that Straffen's mind was both immature and subnormal. He felt that Straffen did not understand the difference between right and wrong and had neither any sense of shame arising from the killings nor any idea of the meaning of guilt. Straffen was suffering from a disease of the mind and was mentally defective, having been certified so on more than one occasion. In addition, he was unable to instruct counsel, since he had no understanding of what counsel was or what it did.

In summing up the evidence, presiding judge Mr Justice Oliver told the jury that 'in this country, we do not try people who are so insane as to not understand what is going on,' pointing out that they might as well try a baby in arms. He asked that the jury find the prisoner insane so that he might deal with him. When the jury complied, the judge ordered that Straffen should be detained during His Majesty's pleasure. Straffen, who had spent his time in custody reading children's comics and adventure stories, was committed to Broadmoor Institution, as it was then known.

Only six months later, in April 1952, he managed to escape. On the pretext of shaking a mat while on cleaning duties, he used a conveniently placed oil drum to climb onto the roof of a shed that was less than 2ft below the height of the perimeter wall. Having climbed onto the wall, he lowered himself carefully onto a fire hydrant box, dropped to the ground and simply walked away. Minutes later, he calmly walked up the drive to the home of Mrs Doris Spencer, whose husband worked at Broadmoor. Having told Mrs Spencer that he was a stranger to the area, he was offered a cup of tea. However, Mrs Spencer's suspicions were aroused when Straffen began to ask questions about Broadmoor, and when he left after fifteen minutes, she immediately telephoned the hospital.

Having left Mrs Spencer's home, Straffen walked for about seven miles before getting a lift with Mrs Dorothy Miles who drove him to a bus stop, from where he could catch a bus into Wokingham. As she alighted from her car, she noticed two warders on bicycles approaching. Straffen also spotted the warders and promptly ran off in the opposite direction. He was recaptured after a brief struggle in a field behind a pub, having been at liberty for just four hours.

Meanwhile, Alice and Roy Simms, the mother and stepfather of a 5-year-old girl, were desperately searching for their daughter, Linda Bowyer. She had gone to play outside on her bicycle earlier in the afternoon and had simply vanished without trace. She was reported missing to police at 10.30 p.m. that evening. Her body was found at dawn the following morning, lying among the bluebells in a copse behind her home. She had been strangled. Almost immediately, the press linked her murder with the escape of John Straffen. When police arrived at Broadmoor to interview him later that day, he indignantly said, 'I know what you policemen are. I know I killed two little children, but I didn't kill the little girl with the bicycle.' Since nobody had mentioned a bicycle at that stage, Straffen was promptly arrested for the murder, all the while protesting, 'That is a frame-up, that is'.

The situation caused the authorities an enormous problem. Logically, Straffen should have been returned to Broadmoor, but the ease of his escape, coupled with his assumed guilt in the murder of Linda Bowyer, put them in an untenable position. When the National Health Service was set up in 1948, responsibility for Broadmoor Institution had passed from the Home Office to the Department of Health. With this change had come a new era of enlightenment. Inmates were now referred to as patients, links with the local community were encouraged and the focus switched from discipline to reform. These changes were not popular in some quarters and there had been demands for Broadmoor to be returned to the control of the Home Office.

To avoid further controversy, Straffen was sent to the hospital wing at Brixton Prison in London, and then taken before magistrates at Reading on 15 May. There the prosecution outlined their case, stating that Linda had been killed at some time between 5.45 p.m. and 6.15 p.m. Since Straffen was recaptured several miles from the murder scene at 6.40 p.m., his defence counsel was quick to argue that he could not have committed the murder in that time frame. However, the magistrates were not swayed by his arguments and committed Straffen to stand trial for the murder of Linda Bowyer.

His trial opened at the Winchester Assizes on 21 July. It was immediately obvious that the Crown carried more weight in the trial than the defence, since the prosecuting counsel was the then solicitor-general, Sir Reginald Manningham-Buller QC. Straffen's lawyer, his opposite number, was not yet a QC and, to further the Crown's case, the chief constables of both Bath and Berkshire and the director of public prosecutions were also present in court. Manningham-Buller's first task was to show that Straffen was now fit to stand trial. The three doctors he called all agreed that Straffen had a mental age of 9½, yet they all declared that he was fit to plead, on the basis that he knew four out of the Ten Commandments.

The prosecution hinged on two strands. The first of these was a request to introduce Straffen's history into the proceedings, drawing on evidence relating to the murders of Brenda Goddard and Cicely Batstone. Until the Criminal Justice Act was revised in 2003, under normal circumstances, a defendant's previous convictions were not disclosed in court prior to the jury's decision. However, in this case, Manningham-Buller argued that since Straffen had not been tried for either murder, then technically they were not convictions and that the striking similarities between all three murders would help to establish the identity of Linda Bowyer's killer. Over the objections of the counsel for the defence, the judge allowed Straffen's previous history to be brought before the court.

Secondly, the prosecution maintained that Straffen could not possibly have known that Linda Bowyer had been riding her bicycle unless he had killed her. His lawyer argued that there had been national publicity about the missing girl and that Straffen could easily have read or been told about the bicycle, or even have guessed what had happened.

At that point, a dramatic turn of events caused the trial to be abandoned. A juror, William Gladwin, admitted to having discussed the case in public, adding that he had studied the maps of the area given to the jurors and formed the opinion that Straffen was not guilty. Rather than ordering Gladwin to stand down and continuing the trial with the remaining eleven jurors, the judge, Mr Justice Cassels, ordered a retrial. By the time a new jury had been sworn in, there had been a large amount of publicity about the case in the national press. Most newspapers had run a photograph on their front pages, showing the mothers of the three murdered girls taking tea together, thus reinforcing the idea in the public conscience that the same man was responsible for the murders of all three.

Straffen was found guilty and sentenced to death, being transferred to the condemned cell at Wandsworth Prison. His conviction was appealed but the appeal was turned down and a date of 4 September 1952 was set for his execution. As the day drew nearer, there was widespread concern over the conviction and sentence. It seemed nonsensical that a man who had only six months before been classed as insane and committed to Broadmoor could now be considered fit to stand trial. On 29 August, Sir David Maxwell-Fyfe, the Home Secretary, granted him a reprieve. Instead of sending him to an institution, Straffen's sentence was commuted to life imprisonment. At the time of writing, he is still incarcerated and still protesting his innocence of the murder of Linda Bowyer.

In the intervening years, new evidence has come to light that casts doubt on Straffen's conviction for Bowyer's murder. Given the time frame in which the murder was committed, new witnesses have been traced who have supported Straffen's story. Several confirm that, at around 5.40 p.m. on the day of the murder, he was some distance away from the scene of the crime – indeed, he was offered a cup of tea by

An illustration of Broadmoor from the Illustrated London News, *August 1867. (© Mary Evans Picture Library)*

one witness and did not finish it until 6 p.m. In fact, Straffen had alibis for almost the entire four-hour period during which he was an escapee.

Several people saw Linda playing on her bicycle at between 5.30 p.m. and 5.50 p.m. and none of these witnesses saw anything unusual. In addition, three witnesses heard what sounded like a child's scream coming from the copse where Linda's body was later found. If this was her final scream, then it occurred at 7 p.m., almost twenty minutes after Straffen had been recaptured.

There were also inconsistencies with the post-mortem report on Linda's body. All three children were manually strangled, none had been sexually assaulted and no attempt had been made to conceal any of the bodies. Dr Robert Teare, who conducted the post-mortem examination of Linda Bowyer, noted the presence of nine crescent-shaped marks on her neck, which he surmised were caused by her killer's fingernails. When police had initially interviewed Straffen at Broadmoor on the morning after Linda's murder, they had tried to take scrapings from beneath his fingernails but could not, as his nails were bitten to the quick.

In the judge's summing up of the case to the jury during Straffen's trial, he had appeared to acknowledge a weakness in the Crown's prosecution case, namely the timing of the killing. If the witnesses for the prosecution were accurate in their estimates of time, then Straffen could not have committed the murder. Moreover, it was uncharacteristic to expect that Straffen, a man who had almost delighted in telling police about the two murders he committed in Somerset, would continue to deny his involvement with the killing of Linda Bowyer.

In 2002, Straffen tried to challenge his life sentence, but his appeal was turned down. He now seems to feel remorse for the murders of Brenda and Cicely, although he continues to protest his innocence of the murder of Linda. Interviewed in 2003, he feels that the man who was responsible for such terrible acts no longer exists and that, after more than fifty years in prison, he has paid his debt to society. John Straffen died on 19 November 2007 in Frankland Prison, County Durham. Aged seventy-seven, he had been incarcerated for more than fifty-five years and was Britain's longest serving prisoner. He continued to deny having murdered Linda Bowyer until his death.

30

'THE STRIFE IS O'ER, THE BATTLE WON'

Loxton, 1954

In 1954, two spinsters, Noreen O'Connor, aged 46, and Friederika Alwine Maria Buls, 77, were sharing a house in the village of Loxton, near Weston-super-Mare. Banker Mr Frank Tiarks, a former director of the Bank of England, had previously employed both women in a domestic capacity.

Miss Buls, known as Marie, had been in service to the Tiarks family for almost fifty years. Of German origin, she had come to England in 1899 to act as a ladies' maid to Frank's wife, Emmy Maria Franziska. When the Second World War began, Miss Buls, a German national, was not permitted to work in England and was interned for the duration of the hostilities. Noreen O'Connor, a state registered nurse, was engaged in her place to care for Mrs Tiarks, who was by now, an invalid. When she died in 1943, O'Connor stayed on to nurse Mr Tiarks, who was confined to a wheelchair after a hunting accident. By the time Miss Buls returned to Loxton after the war, O'Connor was acting as nurse, housekeeper, secretary, chauffeur and general companion to the elderly banker. They frequently attended horse shows and cricket matches together and Miss O'Connor even accompanied her employer on foreign holidays to Persia and South Africa.

When she was not busy working for Mr Tiarks, O'Connor immersed herself in village life, taking a keen interest in the school and helping to raise funds for an extension to the village hall. She was particularly fond of children and would always make homemade chicken broth for any child who fell ill. On the occasion of the wedding of Princess Elizabeth in 1947, she and Tiarks threw a party for the schoolchildren at their home, North Lodge in Loxton, and in June 1954, she assisted with a school trip to Weston-super-Mare.

In 1945, Tiarks had purchased 'Gardeen', an eight-roomed detached cottage in the village of Loxton and gifted it to Noreen O'Connor. He died in 1952, and when his will was read, he had made numerous other bequests to O'Connor, including a £20,000 trust fund, shares and cars. O'Connor moved into Gardeen after his death and asked the increasingly frail Miss Buls to join her. Buls had suffered at least two strokes and by 1954, had also broken her leg, an injury that kept her largely confined to her bedroom. O'Connor nursed her devotedly.

However, at around 7.20 a.m. on Wednesday 1 September 1954, Noreen O'Connor telephoned Peter Tiarks, the youngest son of her late employer. Rousing Peter from his bed, Noreen implored him to come at once as something terrible had happened to Marie and she was in the power of some evil. Tiarks immediately left his home in Bridport, Dorset to drive to Loxton. Less than an hour after the call, Mrs Eva Simmons, the daily help, arrived to begin work at Gardeen. Noticing that the curtains in Marie's bedroom were still closed, she too was told by O'Connor that something terrible had happened. Mrs Simmons assumed that Marie had had another stroke so she did not investigate further.

By the time Peter Tiarks arrived at Gardeen at 10 a.m., Noreen O'Connor was lying peacefully on the sofa in the sitting room, fully clothed. Tiarks asked her what had happened and O'Connor calmly explained that she had seen an evil look in Miss Buls's eyes. This evil look was a regular occurrence whenever Miss Buls looked into a certain corner of the room and, on the previous evening, the look had been so strong that she had plucked out Miss Buls' eyes. Tiarks asked if Marie was dead, to which O'Connor replied; 'I plucked out Marie's eyes but it is not Marie that is dead, it is the evil that was in her.' Horrified, he asked if she realised what she had done, but O'Connor just repeated her assertion that she had merely killed the evil in Miss Buls. Tiarks then sent for a doctor.

Dr Norman Cooper arrived from Winscombe and went upstairs to Miss Buls's bedroom. There he found the old lady lying fully dressed on the floor between her bed and the wall. Her eyeballs had collapsed into her eye sockets and her eyelids, upper lip and right nostril were torn. Cooper estimated that Miss Buls had been dead for between seven and ten hours, and that the cause of her death was shock following the injuries to her face.

Having satisfied himself that Miss Buls was beyond help, Cooper went back downstairs to the sitting room to talk to Noreen. She assured him that there had been a lot of evil things about on the previous evening. She claimed to have heard the sound of drawers being opened and closed and went upstairs to check on her elderly companion. There she formed the impression that Miss Buls did not look herself. As she approached Miss Buls, she had received an electric shock from the old lady's bedspread. She had sat with the woman, whom she felt was in some kind of grave danger, holding her hands and praying, at which point she had heard a strange, disembodied voice saying, 'This is my hate.' She then realised that it was Marie's eyes that were evil and that she had to get them out.

Cooper also asked Noreen if she realised what she had done, to which she maintained that she had simply got rid of evil. In those days, many telephone exchanges were manually operated and, fearful of an operator being able to listen in on his call, Dr Cooper did not pick up the telephone. Instead, he drove three kilometres to the nearest police station at Axbridge to report the crime.

Sergeant Woodriffe arrived and searched Miss Buls's bedroom where he found a tooth, some hair and a broken decorative comb of the kind that was often worn in the hair. He also took a sample of blood from the bedroom floor. In the bathroom he found numerous items of wet clothing, including a dress, an underskirt and a bra. Along with a bloodstained towel found in the bathroom and scrapings from beneath O'Connor's nails, these items were sent to the Forensic Science Laboratory at Bristol. Noreen O'Connor was detained in connection with the death of Miss Buls and taken to the police station at Weston-super-Mare.

There she remained quietly until that evening, when she began to shout, recite religious incantations and move furniture about so that she could kneel and pray.

The police found it necessary to call a doctor to attend her. On the following morning, in the presence of her solicitor, Inspector Leslie Long formally charged Noreen O'Connor with the murder of her companion, Marie Buls. O'Connor took the news calmly, stating that she had no objection at all to telling what had happened and why. She was committed to appear before magistrates at Axbridge Magistrates Court. O'Connor was then transported to Exeter Prison, apparently showing more signs of mental illness on the journey.

Meanwhile, a post-mortem examination was performed on Miss Buls, at which consultant pathologist Dr A.T.F. Rowley found a large bruise on the back of the deceased's head. From this he concluded that it was highly possible that Miss Buls was unconscious at the time her atrocious injuries were received. One of her hands was bloodied and swollen and in it were clutched a few loose hairs.

When O'Connor was brought before the magistrates at Axbridge, the court heard that she and Buls had apparently lived together harmoniously, and O'Connor had been under no obligation under the terms of Mr Tiarks senior's will to allow the old lady to live with her. Neither did O'Connor benefit from Miss Buls's will, a fact that she was well aware of, having been a witness when the will was made. As far as anyone could conceive, O'Connor had no possible motive for wanting Miss Buls dead. Indeed, as Buls grew increasingly old and frail, she had been nursed by the accused with great devotion.

The court was made aware that O'Connor had recently been showing signs of mental illness. Peter Tiarks testified that, in speaking to Noreen on the morning of the gruesome discovery of Miss Buls's body, she had told him about a trip to Plymouth that she had taken on the previous weekend. She had confessed to feeling happy almost to the point of elation and to singing throughout her journey. She had then continued to describe a near-accident experienced on the outing – an accident she was convinced had been engineered by another passenger specifically to cause her death. When the party had taken lunch at Plymouth, it was suggested that they ate at a French restaurant. However, later they decided to take lunch at the Grand Hotel on Plymouth Hoe. Coincidentally, this had been a place at which she had last eaten with Mr Tiarks senior and, when she and her companion were directed to the very same table, she had taken it to mean that her employer was with her in spirit and had intervened to prevent her being taken to a French café. Her behaviour on the trip had been so bizarre that her companion had telephoned her a couple of days later to ask if she was alright.

Tiarks continued to describe O'Connor's account of a parish meeting on the Tuesday evening, stating that by this time. her conversation had become inconsequential and delusional. Questioned about the death of Miss Buls and her part in it, O'Connor did not seem to comprehend what she had done. Indeed, rather than killing her companion, she seemed to believe that she had simply killed something evil and that this was something to be happy about. In her mind, it was not Marie who was dead, but the evil within her.

The magistrates obviously recognised that O'Connor was suffering from some kind of mental illness, but had no other choice than to commit her for trial at the Somerset Assizes. O'Connor had pleaded 'Not Guilty' and, when it was announced that she should stand trial for the murder of Miss Buls, she bowed to the chairman of the bench, Mrs Greenhill, and said quietly 'Thank you, madam.'

The trial opened at Wells on 18 October 1954, lasting just over two hours. Once again, the court heard evidence that O'Connor had been a kindly, very sympathetic and very efficient woman, a pillar of the Loxton community, until her behaviour had become increasingly strange in the period leading up to the murder. Mr Bailey, a former clerk to the Axbridge Rural Council had been one of the last people to see the accused before the events of the night of 31 August/ 1 September.

Noreen O'Connor had visited him at his office during the day and he had asked about her recent trip to Plymouth. She had related her experiences of escape from sudden death and told of eating at the Grand Hotel and her feelings that her late employer was guiding her. Bailey had formed the conclusion that O'Connor was 'mentally deranged'. She revisited his office later that same day and had babbled about several subjects which Bailey felt were nonsensical. At that visit, she had referred to a member of staff as a 'good man', stating that the goodness of his soul was reflected in his eyes. Noreen had asked Bailey if he felt that she had been behaving normally recently, saying, 'If I haven't it will be different now for the evil spirit is dead.' She had then begun to sing the first line of a well-known Easter hymn, 'The strife is o'er, the battle won.' Asked by Bailey if he would see her tomorrow, O'Connor replied that she did not know where she might be tomorrow. She felt so happy that she might go anywhere.

Noreen O'Connor was transferred to Holloway Prison on 25 September and Dr Thomas Christie, the chief medical officer of the prison was called to testify as to her medical condition. It was his opinion that the accused was suffering from an 'acute mania' which had caused defective reasoning. At the time of the murder, this defect of reason was so strong that he believed that she was incapable of knowing that what she was doing was wrong. Dr Desmond Curran, a psychiatrist based at St George's Hospital, London, backed his opinion. Curran also felt it highly improbable that O'Connor knew what she was doing when she murdered Miss Buls.

Norman Skelhorn, acting for the defence, summed up the situation for the jury. He stressed that there was no motive, financial or otherwise, for the murder of Marie Buls. He reiterated that it was unlikely that Miss Buls had suffered the terrible pain of her horrific injuries, since the medical opinion was that she was unconscious before they were inflicted, either as a result of a blow to the head, which was supported by the large bruise found at the post-mortem, or by having succumbed to a heart attack or another stroke. Inflicting the injuries was something that was completely foreign to the nature of the accused, who was known to be a kind, friendly person and a devoted and efficient nurse.

In his concluding remarks the presiding judge, Mr Justice Byrne, advised the jury that if they were satisfied with the evidence, they would have no doubt that Miss O'Connor was guilty of the murder of Miss Buls. However, he asked them to consider the second aspect of the case that according to medical opinion, the accused was unaware of what she was doing, or if she did know, then she did not know it was wrong. If they thought she was guilty then he advised them that the correct verdict would be 'Guilty but insane'.

The jury did not need to retire to consider the evidence further. In only a minute, they delivered their verdict, finding Noreen O'Connor guilty of the murder of Marie Buls, but insane, leaving Mr Justice Byrne, to direct that she be detained at Broadmoor Special Institution at Her Majesty's pleasure.

It is believed that Noreen O'Connor was eventually released from Broadmoor, spending the remainder of her life as an in-patient at St Andrew's Hospital, Northampton, a charitable organisation devoted to the care of patients with mental disorders, learning disabilities and acquired brain injuries, and she died there in 1983.

BIBLIOGRAPHY & REFERENCES

Where individual newspapers or journal articles have been consulted for specific cases, these are cited in the list below. Most of the books that follow have been consulted in the research for several chapters.

NEWSPAPER & JOURNAL REFERENCES

1. 'Good people, pray for me!', 1740
Sherborne Mercury, 22 April 1740

3. 'I am entirely innocent',1823
Sherborne Journal, 24 August 1825
Western Flying Post, 3 March–7 April 1823

4. 'There are thieves in the house!', 1828
The Times, 4 February 1828
Taunton Courier, 13 February, 11 June 1828

5. 'Not a fortnight longer! Mark my words', 1829
North Devon Journal Herald, 3 September 1829
Taunton Courier, 15 July–2 September 1829

6. 'Here's a pretty bitch coming down the lane', 1829
Bath Journal, 7 December 1829
Sherborne Journal, 31 December 1829, 15 April and 22 April 1830
Taunton Courier, 9 and 29 December 1829, 14 and 21 April, 15 May, 23 June 1830

7. 'Neither a murder nor a mystery', 1830
Taunton Courier, 18 and 25 August, 2 and 15 September 1830
Western Flying Post, 16 and 30 August, 6 September 1830

10. 'What Martha's already said goes for nothing', 1843
Sherborne Mercury, 19 August 1843
Somerset County Gazette, 19 August 1843

BIBLIOGRAPHY & REFERENCES

11. 'It's no use, I've done it', 1844
Western Flying Post, 8 June, 17 August and 7 September 1844

12. 'Ask her first if she believes in God?', 1851
Bath Chronicle, 16 and 23 October 1851, 8 April 1852
Taunton Courier, 22 October 1851
Western Flying Post, 14 and 21 October 1851, 6 April 1852

13. 'I did it for love', 1851
The Times, 29 October 1851, 8 April 1852, 19 and 23 September, 10 October 1861
Bath Chronicle, 30 October, 6 November 1851
Western Flying Post, 7 and 28 October 1851
News of the World, 26 October and 2 November 1851
Taunton Courier, 9 and 16 October 1861

14. 'We'll find the body yet', 1858
The Times, 8 January 1859
Taunton Courier, 12 January 1859

15. 'Nothing has ever been administered to her in her food', 1860
Western Flying Post, 31 July and 4 September 1860

16. 'No one knew of my intention', 1860
The Times, 21 and 28 July, 14 August, 2 October 1860; 9 April 1861; 26–27 April, 1 and 5 May, 29 June, 28 August 1865
Western Flying Post, 10, 24 and 31 July, 9 and 16 October, 13 November 1860, 5 February 1861

17. 'Spare my wife', 1861
Taunton Courier, 16 January, 27 March, 10 April 1861

19. 'Goodnight', 1883
Taunton Courier, 17 and 24 January, 14 February 1883
Western Gazette, 25 May 1883

20. 'Yes, I done it!', 1883
Western Gazette, 6 and 13 April, 25 May 1883

21. 'You ought to be hanged', 1889
The Times, 14 January, 21 and 22 February 1889

22. 'You will have me here for something more serious than this', 1913
Bridgwater Mercury, 8 January 1913

24. 'Go on, put down what you like', 1933
Western Gazette, 2 March, 28 July 1933

25. 'I shall be glad when the old bastard is out of the way', 1933
Bath Weekly Chronicle, 9 December 1933, 5 May 1934

26. 'Stop worrying. It is all right', 1943
Master Detective Magazine, December 1998
Western Gazette, November 1943–March 1944

27. 'Thank you', 1947
Bridgwater Mercury, 16 and 23 September, 2, 16 and 23 December 1947, 6 January 1948

28. 'One of the most terrible cases of murder I have known', 1950
Bridgwater Mercury, 18 and 25 April, 2 May 1950
Burnham On Sea Gazette, 28 April, 2 June 1950

29. 'That is a frame-up, that is', 1951–2
Bath Weekly Chronicle and Herald, 21 and 28 July, 4, 11, 18 and 25 August, 1 September, 20 October 1951
The Scotsman, 29 May 2002
The Daily Telegraph, 27 May 2001
The Times, 29 September 2005

30. 'The strife is o'er, the battle won', 1954
Wells Journal and West of England Advertiser, September–October 1954

BOOKS

Byford, Enid, *Somerset Murders*, Dovecote Press, 1990
Evans, Roger, *Somerset Tales of Mystery and Murder*, Countryside, 2004
Eddleston, John J., *The Encyclopedia of Executions*, John Blake, 2004
Fielding, Steve, *The Hangman's Record, Vol. 1, 1868–1899; Vol. 2, 1900–1929; Vol. 3, 1930–1964*, CBD, 1994–2005
Hurley, Jack, *Murder and Mystery on Exmoor*, Exmoor Press, 1982
Norris, Sally, *Tales of old Somerset*, Newbury, Countryside, 1999
Sweet, Jack W., *Shocking Somerset Murders*, Somerset Books, 2000
Wilson, Colin, introduced by, *Murder in the Westcountry*, Bossiney, 1975
Worthy, David, *A Quantock tragedy: The Walford murder of 1789*, Friam Press, 1998

INDEX

Abrahams, John 38
A'court, John 41–2
Aldridge, Dr Russell 74–6
Alford, Dr H. J. 104
Alvin, Richard 45–51
Anning, Robert 41–2
Ashford, Mr 64
Atkin, Mr Justice 114
Atwell, Ronald Douglas 134–6
Atyeo, Alice & Francesca 106–11
Atyeo, Frank 107–11
Avis, Arthur 100

Bagnall, Maria 17–21
Bailey Smith, James 55
Baker, Peter 53
Bath, 17, 19, 58, 61, 121, 137
Batstone, Cicely 139–43
Benger, Thomas 79
Bennet, Det. Inspector 117
Bernard, Mr 54–5
Berry, James 105
Biss, Lawrence 33–7
Bowdage, Emmanuel 46, 50
Bowers, Emily 131–3
Bowyer, Linda 141–3
Bragg, Robert & John 29
Branch, Betty 1–4
Branch, Elizabeth, 1–4
Branch, Parry & Benjamin 1
Brewer, Doris 116–20
Brewer, Lily 119
Bridgwater 134
Bridgwater Gaol 25
Bristol Assizes 133

Brixton Prison 141
Broadmoor 140–3, 148
Buckland St Mary 11–6
Bucknall, John Charles 83
Budd (family) 1–4
Bulgin, Elizabeth 102
Bulgin, Sarah 45–6
Buls, Friederika 144–8
Burgess, Anna Maria 67–72
Burgess, Catherine 24
Burgess, William 67–72
Burrough, Sir James 16
Buttesworth, Jane 1–4
Byrne, Mr Justice 148

Caines, Richard 37, 38, 42
Calcraft, William 72, 89
Carpenter, Dr J.S. 123, 124
Carter, Dr Godfrey 116, 118
Carter, Mary Ann 28, 29
Cassels, Mr Justice 142
Castle of Comfort 7, 8
Chant, George 91–4
Chard 11, 26, 33
Chillington Common 33
Clark, Hugh 36
Clarke, Geoffrey 117
Clarke, Martha 45–51
Clarke, Mrs 30
Cockburn, Mr 50–1
Cole, Mr 92–3
Coleridge, Mr Justice 42, 50–2, 83
Coles, Arnold 42, 43
Coles, Charlotte 46–8
Collyns, Mr 23–5 Colmer, Ann 25
Cooper, Dr Norman 145–8

Cottle, Elizbeth 37
Cowley, Mrs 139
Cox, Mark 96–8
Cox, Mr 15
Cox, Sarah 79
Coxe, Mrs 17–21
Crewkerne 45, 77
Crocker, William 41–4
Crosby, Thomas 59–62
Culliford, PC 101
Curry Mallet 116, 117
Curry Rivel 37

Davies, Arthur 103
Davies, Emma Jane 103–5
Davies, George 103–5
Davis, Charles 37
Dawe, William 44
Dawkins, James 19
Dead Woman's Ditch 5–10
Dewhurst, Mr 132
Digby, Dawn 126–130
Digby, Ernest 126–130
Doddington 7
Drewett, Sperintendent John 97–8
Dundry 85

Erle, Mr Justice 62
Erle, William 28–32
Etheredge, Alfred 41, 42
Eustace, Mr 35
Evans, Evan 59
Evans, Mary 53–5
Exeter Prison 114, 116

Ffooks, Mr 92–4
Fisher, Joel 52–7

INDEX

Fisher, Mary (*née* Hyatt) 52–7
Flood, William 12–6
Ford, PC 124
Fowler, Mary 46–51
Fraser, Dr 125
Frome 1, 3, 63, 64, 78

Gagg, John 82
Garland, Dr 73–6, 91–4
Garland Robert, 99
Gaselee, Mr Justice 31, 32
Gibbs, Edith 126, 127
Gibson, Charles 136
Giles, Mr 63–4
Gillham, Richard 17–21
Gladwin, William 142
Goddard, Brenda 138–143
Goddard, Lord Chief Justice 133
Gough, Elizabeth 79, 80, 83
Gould, Fred 99–102
Grant, Elizabeth 59–62
Greedy, PC Joseph 114–5

Habbefield, John 97
Hann, Edwin 100
Hansford, George 90–4
Harp, Thomas & William 27
Harris, Edmund & Charles 35
Harvey, John 37–40
Hawkins, Dr C.F. 107
Hebditch, Benjamin 33–7
Hemington 1, 3
Henstridge 99
Herapath, Professor William 60–2, 73–4
Hewlett, Joseph 55
Hill, Olga Davy 126–130
Hill, Robert 54–5
Hinks, Constance Ann (nee Pullen, formerly Jeffries) 121–5
Hinks, Reginald Ivor 121–5
Hoare, John 38–40

Holloway Prison 147
Holly, Esther 80
Horfield Prison 120, 125, 136, 137, 140
Howe, William 38–40
Hubbard, William 90–4
Huddleston, Baron 98, 102
Huish, Robert 114
Hurd, Robert 63–5
Hyatt, Thomas 57

Ilchester Gaol 4, 14, 15, 21, 25, 28, 32, 39, 40
Ilminster 104, 117

Jeddard, Mr Justice 118
Jeffs, Superintendent 69
Jurkiewicz, Eugenius 131–3

Keats, Benjamin 90–4
Keevil, John 85–9
Kent, Constance Emily 77–84
Kent, Edward 78
Kent, Mary Ann 77
Kent, Mary Drewe (*née* Pratt) 77–84
Kent, Samuel Savill 77–84
Kent, Savill 77–84
Kent, William 77–84
Kenyon, Lord Chief Justice 8
Kinglake, Mr 42–3

Langport 37, 39
Lawrence, John 1–4
Lawrence, Mr 59–61
Leach, Henry 41
Lewis, Elizabeth (aka Slater) 58–62
Lewis, Mr 131
Long, Dr Robert Godolphin 101, 102
Long, William 30
Lovell, William 86
Loveridge, Mr 46
Loxton 144–8

Lucy, Margaret 36
Lyons, Eliza 59–60

Maggs, William 63–5
Manningham-Buller, Sir Reginald 141, 142
Mao, Francis 27
Marley, Mrs 68–71
Marsh, Honor 15
Marshall, Bessie 95–6
Martin, Baron 89
Matthews, Susan 34
Maxwell-Fyfe, Sir David 143
Middleton, Alice 113–13
Middlezoy 131–3
Milborne Port 126
Miles, Dorothy 141
Milett, Stephen 79
Moate, Geoffrey 134
Moore, John 74, 76
Morrison, Herbert 130
Morse, Frederick 116–120
Morse, Harold 115, 116
Mullett, William 99, 102

Nether Stowey 5–10
Norman, William 16
Norris, Inspector John 59, 62
Norris, Robert 27, 33
North Petherton 106–11

O'Connor, Noreen 144–8
Old Bailey 125
Oliver, Mr Justice 136, 140
Over Stowey 5–10
Over Stratton, 33

Palmer, Lily Irene 134–6
Parks, Dr 140
Pattison, Mr Justice 39, 55, 56
Payne, James 66
Peacock, Revd Dr 80
Pearce, Charles & Mercy 95
Pearce, Emma 95–7
Peedon, Mary 30
Peel, Sir Robert 31, 32

INDEX

Penny, William 90–4
Perry, Robert 33, 34
Peters, Sarah 73–6
Peters, Silvester 73–6
Phillips, Cyril 106–10
Philips, Henry 41
Pierrepoint, Thomas 114, 120, 125, 130
Porlock 112–14
Pottinger, William 46
Pugsley, Henry & Fanny 112–14
Pullen, Doris & Arthur 138, 139
Pullen, James 121–5

Quartly, Henry 111–14
Quick, Ann 22–4

Reed, Abraham 22–5
Reed, Mary 22–5
Reyland, Samuel 103–5
Rice, Ann 5–10
Rice, George 6
Rio, Mary 12
Rist's Lace Factory 27–32
Roach, Charles Tucker, Elizabeth & Jessy 110
Road / Rode 77
Rogers, Charles 91–4
Russell, John 27–32

Salisbury, Joseph 27
Sandpit Hill, 37
Searle, Mr & Mrs 58–62
Seer, Joseph 65
Sellick, Ellen 106, 107
Shepton Mallet Gaol 21, 66, 105, 114
Shortland, John 86
Simmonds, Hugh 46
Simms, Alice & Roy 141
Simonsbath 67
Singleton, Mr Justice 130
Slater, Elizabeth 58-2
Smith, Elizabeth 124

Smith, William 35
Somers, Ann 1–4
South Molton 89
Sparrow, William 63–5
Spencer, Doris 141
Spicer, Northcote 27
Spilsbury, Sir Bernard 117
St Andrews Hospital 148
Stanbrook, Sgt Mjr Charles 100, 101
Standert, Hugh 24
Stoneman, Robert 24
Straffen, John 137–43
Strong, Elizabeth 106
Stuckey, Simeon 30, 33–6
Summers, Jacob & Joan 26
Sweet, Jack 32
Sylvester, Mr 35

Taunton 116, 140
Taunton Assizes 21, 61
Taunton Gaol 56, 72, 89, 98, 102
Taylor, Arthur 109, 110
Templer Pole, Sir William 15
Thatcher, Alfred 95–6
Thorne, John 23
Thornton, Revd William 67–72
Tiarks, Frank, Emmy & Peter 144–8
Tomkyns, Dr 76
Touchays 26, 27
Trump, Betty 11–6
Trump, Samuel & Elizabeth 11–6
Tugwell, G.H. 20
Turner, Joan 27–32
Turner, John & Elizabeth 45–50

Upsall, William 54

Wade, 130
Wagner, Rev Arthur 82
Walford, Ann 6

Walford, Jane (*née* Shorney) 5–10
Walford, John 5-10
Walford's Gibbet 10
Walter, Winter 73–4
Wandsworth Prison 143
Warry, Dr Taylor 74–6
Waterman, George & Sarah 85–9
Waterman, Thomas 87, 89
Watkins, George 41–4
Watts, John & Leah 63
Watts, Sarah 63–6
Webber, William 71
Webster, Prof J.M. 129
Wedlake, Job 97–8
Wedlake, Joseph 95–8
Wedlake, Thomas 96–8
Wedmore, Charles 87–9
Wedmore, Matthew 87–9
Wedmore, William 87, 88
Wells, 56, 114, 134, 147
West, Richard 108
West Coker 91, 94
Westcott, John & Henry 24
West Hatch 116–20
Weston-super-Mare 52, 146
Whicher, Jonathan 80–2
White, Clara 99–102
White, George 99–102
White, Harriet 26
Wick St Lawrence 52
Williams, Supt William 108
Wills, Mr Justice 104
Wincanton 101
Winchester Assizes 141
Windwhistle Inn 33
Winsham 11
Withypool 22
Wyatt, Philip 15 Wybrants, Dr 91

Yeobridge 103
Yeovil 41, 73, 90, 127